HOTSPOTS
COSTA

Written by Donna Dailey; updated by Marc Di Duca

Published by Thomas Cook Publishing
A division of Thomas Cook Tour Operations Limited.
Company registration no. 1450464 England
The Thomas Cook Business Park, Unit 9, Coningsby Road,
Peterborough PE3 8SB, United Kingdom
Email: sales@thomascook.com, Tel: + 44 (0) 1733 416477
www.thomascookpublishing.com

Produced by Cambridge Publishing Management Limited
Burr Elm Court, Main Street, Caldecote CB23 7NU
ISBN13: 978-1-84157-852-1

First edition © 2006 Thomas Cook Publishing
This second edition © 2008
Text © Thomas Cook Publishing,
Maps © Thomas Cook Publishing/PCGraphics (UK) Limited

Series Editor: Diane Ashmore
Production/DTP: Steven Collins

Printed and bound in Spain by GraphyCems

Cover photography © SIME/Schmid Reinhard

CONTENTS

WHAT'S IN YOUR GUIDEBOOK?

Independent authors Impartial, up-to-date information from our travel experts who meticulously source local knowledge.

Experience Thomas Cook's 165 years in the travel industry and guidebook publishing enriches every word with expertise you can trust.

Travel know-how Contributions by thousands of staff around the globe, each one living and breathing travel.

Editors Travel-publishing professionals, pulling everything together to craft a perfect blend of words, pictures, maps and design.

You, the traveller We deliver a practical, no-nonsense approach to information, geared to how you really use it.

● *Benidorm, Costa Blanca*

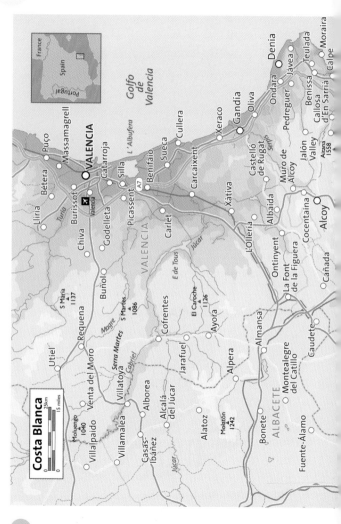

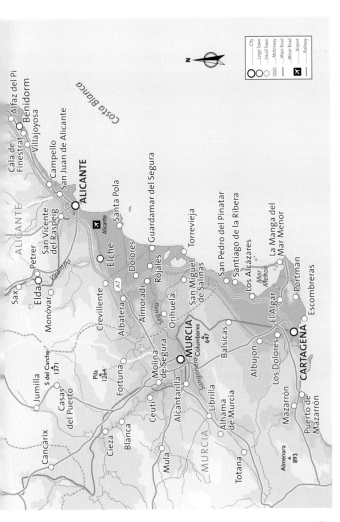

Map legend:
- City
- Large Town
- Small Town
- Motorway
- Main Road
- Minor Road
- Airport
- Railway

N

Costa Blanca

Alfaz del Pi
Benidorm
Villajoyosa
Cala de Finestrat
Campello
San Juan de Alicante
ALICANTE
Petrer
San Vicente del Raspeig
Sax
Elda
Monóvar
ALICANTE
Vinalopó
Santa Pola
Elche
A7
Crevillente
Dolores
Guardamar del Segura
Torrevieja
San Pedro del Pinatar
Almoradí
Rojales
San Miguel de Salinas
Santiago de la Ribera
La Manga del Mar Menor
Albatera
Segura
Orihuela
Los Alcázares
Mar Menor
Portman
Jumilla
S del Carche
1371
Casas del Puerto
Pila
1264
Fortuna
Molina de Segura
MURCIA
Columbares
647
Balsicas
El Algar
Escombreras
CARTAGENA
Cancárix
Cieza
Blanca
Ceuti
Sangonera
Alcantarilla
Librilla
Albujon
Los Dolores
Mula
Alhama de Murcia
MURCIA
Mazarrón
Puerto de Mazarrón
Totana
Almenara
893

7

Getting to know the Costa Blanca

The Costa Blanca – the 'White Coast' – was christened 2,500 years ago by Greek traders who founded the colony of Akra Leuka ('White Headland') near today's Alicante. It is a paradise of blue skies, superb beaches, and sun that shines nearly every day of the year. Amid the rocky, sunbaked landscape are fertile river valleys, lush groves of oranges, lemons, olives and almonds, and vineyards producing sweet muscatel grapes.

The Costa Blanca is part of the region of Valencia, which is broken into smaller localities including La Marina Alta (Jávea and Denia), La Marina Baixa (Benidorm) and Alicante. Each has its own special gastronomy, crafts and fiestas, creating a *calderón* (melting pot) of delightful surprises.

Above all, visitors come to the Costa Blanca for sun and sea. There are 37 Blue Flag beaches – a mark of clean water and top facilities – along this stretch of coast, more than in any other European tourist destination. Some clever soul has worked out that the sun shines on the Costa Blanca for more than 2,600 hours every year.

The Costa Blanca has amazing natural beauty lying just behind its beaches. A range of rugged mountains and sculpted peaks creates a spectacular backdrop, less than an hour's drive away. The small villages where life carries on as it has for centuries are a stark contrast to the hedonistic beach scene. In between the terraced mountainsides are valleys fragrant with flowers and wild herbs. Sometimes the mountains wade into the sea, creating tranquil coves beneath precipitous cliffs and landmarks like the striking Peñón de Ifach (see page 23).

MOORISH NAMES

After the Christian re-conquest, many Moors continued to inhabit towns here, until they were officially expelled in 1609. Inland towns still bear traces of this in their ruined castles, architecture and even names: the prefix 'Beni', means 'son of' in Arabic.

On the Costa Blanca there are all sorts of watersports on offer, with several golf courses, and opportunities for adventure sports such as rock-climbing. A wander around one of the old town centres will reveal charming squares, parish churches, narrow streets of immaculate, whitewashed houses or others lined with imposing medieval mansions. There are many ways to explore the Costa Blanca; on coach tours, boat trips, trams, trains and, of course, you can always hire a car.

Fiestas are the heart and soul of the Costa Blanca. Giant statues are set aflame in the town squares, bulls jump into the sea and latter-day Moors and Christians re-enact historic battles, while small local fiestas are marked by costumes, processions and dancing. The Spanish celebrate with dedication and style, and there are festivities around the Costa Blanca at almost any time of year.

COSTA BLANCA IN THE PAST

The Iberians, Greeks and Romans all had settlements on the Costa Blanca, but its strongest influence came from the Arabic Moors, who landed at Gibraltar in AD 711 and held sway over southern Spain for nearly 800 years. They introduced citrus fruits, rice, dates, cotton, and irrigation and terrace farming, which enabled the Costa Blanca to thrive.

The other influence on the Costa Blanca was the sea. Coastal villages were often prey to pirate attack, and fortress-churches and windows with heavy, iron grilles are still in evidence, along with busy fishing ports.

COSTA BLANCA TODAY

The 1950s and 1960s saw the start of tourist development here. Benidorm, long a British favourite, is mainland Spain's largest resort; from a distance, its high-rise skyline shimmers like a mirage. Benidorm would be a sleepy town of 57,000 were it not for the annual influx of 3.5 million visitors, a third of whom are British. Bitter, *Guinness* and the English breakfast sit side by side with *San Miguel* and local dishes. Do not expect everyone to speak English, however. There is an increasing number of visitors from the rest of Europe. The locals speak Valencian, one of the country's four main languages, which is similar to Catalan.

THE BEST OF THE COSTA BLANCA

TOP 10 ATTRACTIONS

- **Best beaches** Try the Playa Arenal at Jávea (see page 15), Denia's 12 km (7½ miles) of coastline (see page 57) or Benidorm's Playa de Levante (see page 25).

- **Best views** Some of the best views are Peñón de Ifach (see page 21), Benidorm's twin beaches form the castle mirador (see page 25) and Benidorm's skyline seen on a boat trip to Isla de Benidorm (see page 30).

- **Guadelest** The eagle's-nest village of Guadelest is extraordinary (see page 69).

- **Alicante's Explanada de España** This must be the prettiest stroll on the Costa Blanca (see page 76).

- **Medieval Benissa** This traditional inland town is largely unaffected by tourism and has retained its medieval and Moorish architecture (see page 65).

🔻 Altea boasts a church with unique blue-and-white tiled domes

- Step back in time in **Calle Purissima** in **Benissa**. Take a walk up here and the surrounding streets to get a glimpse of Spanish life past and present (see page 65).

- **Altea's Plaza de la Iglesia** and its steep old streets make an atmospheric stop to while away the hours (see page 67).

- **Fonts de l'Algar** Imagine yourself as part of a postcard picture beside the magical pools and waterfalls here (page 71).

- **Best theme parks** Visit **Aqualandia** – the biggest water park in Europe and among the best in the world (see pages 26 and 102). For more excitement, visit **Terra Mítica** – Benidorm's top tourist attraction and one of Europe's best theme parks (see pages 28 and 103).

- **Nightlife** Don't miss the glitzy extravaganza of music and dance at **Benidorm Palace** (see page 34).

SYMBOLS KEY

The following symbols are used throughout this book:

📍 address   📞 telephone   🌐 website address   ✉ email

🕐 opening times   ⓘ important

The following symbols are used on the maps:

Ⓜ metro stop

ⓘ information office

✉ post office

🛍 shopping

✈ airport

➕ hospital

🏠 police station

🚌 bus station

🚊 railway station

✝ church

○ city

○ large town

○ small town

■ poi (point of interest)

▬ motorway

— main road

— minor road

— railway

RESTAURANT CATEGORIES

The symbol after the name of each restaurant listed in this guide indicates the price of a typical three-course meal without drinks for one person:

£ budget price   ££ mid-range price   £££ most expensive

🔴 numbers denote featured cafés, restaurants & evening venues

◐ *Beach and Peñón de Ifach, Calpe*

RESORTS
Places under the sun

◆ *Jávea's hilly outlook*

Jávea

Running between two headlands – Cap Sant Antoni to the north and Cap de la Nao to the south, both with splendid views – Jávea, also known as Xábia in the local language (Castillian), sparkles with signs of the good life. Pockets of orange trees or pine forest conceal smart residential zones hidden in the hills.

BEACHES

The best swimming beach is the wide, sandy, **Playa Arenal**, with shallow water and gentle waves. In the evening, local artisans set up a good crafts market along the promenade. Playa de la Grava is a narrow, pebbly beach stretching out from Jávea's small port. Halfway along, the large rock ledge jutting out into the sea makes a peaceful spot. The pretty, tiled promenade is a nice place to join the locals for a late afternoon or evening stroll.

THINGS TO SEE & DO

Cap de la Nao
A pretty coastal drive south of Jávea takes you to the lighthouse at Cap de la Nao. From the lighthouse you will have a good look at the precipitous headland and misty views of the distant mountains. There are a couple of bar-restaurants for refreshments. Back on the main road, you can carry on to Granadella, passing through a forest with shady spots for a picnic. The area is popular for hiking. The road ends at the tiny village, where there is an equally tiny – but very busy – pebble beach of large, white stones. It has a beach bar, sunbeds and thatched umbrellas.

Cap Sant Antoni
From the Old Town, take Calle Virgen de Los Angeles (signposted to Denia), and turn right at the top of the hill after a series of winding curves (signposted). There is a lighthouse at the end of the road, and viewpoints with great views over Jávea's port, beach and bay.

The Old Town

At the heart of Jávea's Old Town is the Gothic fortress church of San Bartolomé, surrounded by medieval houses. The archaeological museum has a small but good collection of artefacts spanning several eras, and is housed in a beautiful 17th-century mansion.

Museum ⓐ Calle Primicas ❶ 96 579 1098 ❷ 10.00–13.00 & 18.00–21.00 Mon–Fri, 10.00–13.00 Sat & Sun ❶ Admission free. A good place to pick up tasty cheeses and cold meats is the **indoor market** ❷ 08.00–13.30 & 17.00–21.00 Mon–Fri, 08.00–14.00 Sat, closed Sun

SHOPPING

Cristobel Specialists in fine-quality, engraved glassware. ⓐ Corner of Calle Roques and M Gallard, across from the municipal market ❶ 96 646 0257 ❷ 09.30–13.30 & 17.00–20.00 Mon–Fri, 09.30–13.30 Sat

Decuero Handmade belts, bags, wallets and leather goods, some handpainted. ⓐ Plaça de la Iglesia in the Old Town ❶ 96 579 3706 ❷ Closed Sat afternoon and Sun

Jakarta One of the best gift shops on the Costa Blanca. Stylish sun-dresses, T-shirts, skirts and trendy beachwear. Arty gifts such as painted wooden cats, decorative mirrors, great jewellery. ⓐ Paseo Amanecer, Playa Arenal ❶ 96 579 3851

Mercadona Jávea's biggest supermarket ⓐ Avenida de Pla, the main road between the Old Town and Arenal

La Pallissa Lladró, glassware, dolls, mirrors and comical statues and figurines. ⓐ Paseo Amanecer, Playa Arenal ❶ 96 647 0618 ❷ Closed Sun

Polly's Bookshop A good selection of secondhand English books. ⓐ Across from the port tourist office ❷ 10.00–13.30 & 17.00–19.30 Mon–Sat, closed Sun

Children

Every evening, there is a funfair with games and rides on Paseo Amanecer, opposite the Arenal beach. Next door is a small go-karting track. Or catch the tourist train (evenings) for a ride around town.

TAKING A BREAK

El Clavo £ Authentic fishermen's bar at the port, serving tapas and fresh fish; this place is well worth a try. ⓐ Bastarreche 15 ⓣ 96 579 1014 ⓛ Lunch & dinner; closed Wed

Tasca Tonis £ Good regional home cooking using fresh local produce makes this busy restaurant an area favourite. ⓐ Major 2 ⓣ 96 646 1851 ⓛ Closed Sun afternoon

Restaurante Cristóbal Colón £–££ This busy beachside restaurant features fresh fish caught in the local bay. There is a menu of the day and cheap chicken and spaghetti dishes for children. ⓐ Playa Arenal ⓣ 96 647 0958 ⓛ 12.30–17.00, 19.00–24.00; closed Nov and Dec

Calima ££ The pick of the bunch on the seafront, where you can feast on monkfish, sea bass, suckling pig, duck or rabbit in the simple whitewashed and tiled interior or out on the promenade just metres from the surf. ⓐ Avenida Mediterráneo 14 ⓣ 96 579 4821 ⓛ 19.30–24.00

L'Hellin ££ Set alongside the town's pebble beach, enjoy a cool drink on the terrace of this popular café bar followed by light Mediterranean fare. ⓐ Avenida Mediterráneo ⓣ 96 579 1379 ⓛ 12.30–16.00 & 19.00–23.00 Thur–Tues June–Oct

Puerto ££ Enjoy a large selection of local meat and fish dishes or paella directly above the crashing waves of the Med. Best sea views of any eatery in town from the balcony. ⓐ Explanada del puerto ⓣ 96 579 1064 ⓛ 12.00–16.00 & 20.00–24.00

Casita de Paco ££–£££ The speciality here is *fideua*, a regional dish of tiny spaghetti cooked in a fish stock. ⓐ Jávea–Gata road, just before Benitachell crossing ⓣ 96 579 5909 ⓛ Closed Tues winter

AFTER DARK

La Llum One of Jávea's hottest night spots attracting a younger crowd. ⓐ Carrer de Gual 1 ⓛ 18.00–04.00

Moli Blanc The 'white windmill' disco is huge inside, with an open-air bar and a swimming pool. ⓐ Calle del Cabo de la Nao ⓣ 96 579 0507 ⓛ 23.00–06.00 Fri and Sat all year, nightly in summer ⓘ Admission charge

Montgó di Bongo Caters for the beach crowd by day, smart dress in the evening. ⓐ Playa de la Grava ⓛ July and Aug only

⬤ *Jávea harbour*

Moraira

Moraira is a small gem of a resort situated between Jávea and Calpe. A handful of streets rises up behind a pretty yacht-filled harbour. Between the port and the sandy l'Ampolla beach are the remains of an old Moorish castle and a tiny chapel. On the other side of the port, below the Torre-vigía (the old stone watchtower), on top of Cap d'Or, is El Portet, a Blue Flag beach that is good for watersports.

The tourist information office is located on the Moraira–Calpe road, opposite the beach. ☎ 96 574 5168

TAKING A BREAK

El Andaluz ££ Regional cuisine and barbecue. Live jazz music and Flamenco shows in summer. ⓐ Calle Pintor El Greco 7 ☎ 96 574 5729 🕐 12.30–16.00 & 20.00–late

Girasol £££ It is worth the drive into the hills above Moraira to eat at one of the best restaurants in Spain. The superb Mediterranean cuisine is matched only by the views over the hills and coast from the terrace.

SHOPPING
There is a lively fish market every morning at the port from 10.00.
Bodega Carmen Good selection of wines and liqueurs, with little gift bottles of muscatel and other spirits. ⓐ Calle Dr Calatayud 28 🕐 09.00–14.00 & 17.00–21.00, closed Sun evening
Ceramica Les Sorts Well-stocked treasure trove of brightly hued pottery from around the region. ⓐ Edif Kristal Mar 18D–18E ☎ 96 574 5737
Vicente Ferrer Fun and unique gifts – photo frames, dolls, ceramics, crafts, kitchenware. ⓐ Calle Dr Calatayud 41 ☎ 96 574 4053 🕐 Closed Sun evening (summer); closed Sat evening and Sun (winter)

ⓐ Carretera Moraira–Calpe km 1.5 ⓣ 96 574 4373 ⓛ Dinner only
July–Aug; lunch and dinner, but closed Sun evening & Mon Sept–June

La Sort ££££ Stylish, contemporary design and a menu of international
nouvelle cuisine creations with a heavy Spanish twist make this
family-run restaurant a place to dress up for. ⓐ Avenida Madrid 1
ⓣ 96 649 1161 ⓛ 13.00–16.00 & 19.00–23.00

🔺 *Moraira's marina has some great restaurants*

Calpe

Calpe is dominated by the **Peñón de Ifach**, the majestic natural landmark of the Costa Blanca shoreline. This volcanic rock rises more than 300 m (990 ft) above sea level, like a mini Rock of Gibraltar, and is joined to the mainland by a narrow strip of land. Calpe is a large, busy resort and at first glance its skyline of modern hotel development obscures its origins as an ancient fishing village. Early Iberian tribes settled here, and the Romans founded a prosperous colony.

The port, at the foot of Ifach, is always bustling with fishing boats and pleasure craft, and there are pleasant bars and cafés from which to enjoy the scene. Watch the trawlers return to port after a day at sea to sell their catch at the lively fish auction. In the Old Town centre you can see typical fishermen's houses along the streets.

BEACHES

Calpe has three good sandy beaches. La Fossa-Levante lies at the base of Ifach, running north and east into the next beach, Playa Calalga. The third, Playa Arenal–Bol, runs west from the port to the Old Town.

THINGS TO SEE & DO

Museo Fester (Fiestas Museum)
On show here is a variety of Calpe's colourful costumes and decorations, including those from the Moors and Christians, the Fallas and other celebrations.
ⓐ Calle José Antonio ⓣ 96 583 9123 ⓛ 10.30–13.30 & 18.00–22.00 summer; 17.00–20.00 Tues–Sun winter ⓘ Admission free

The Old Town
Calpe's Old Town reveals glimpses of its history and culture. Torreón de la Peça is a defence tower reinforced by the remains of the Old Town walls. Attached to the attractive parish church is the Iglesia Antigua, the

⬥ *A street in Calpe's Old Town*

region's only standing example of the Gothic-Mudejar architectural style. Near the church is a small **archaeological museum**.
🕐 10.30–13.30 & 18.00–22.00 summer; 17.00–20.00 Tues–Sun winter
ℹ️ Admission free. Arrabal is the old Moorish quarter of steep, narrow streets and small, whitewashed houses; the pavement stones display anchors, geometrical drawings and other motifs typical of Calpe.

Peñón de Ifach

The towering rock has been turned into a nature park. Peregrine falcons and a large colony of seagulls nest in the rock walls. The **Nature Room** contains exhibits about the park. You can climb to the summit (allow up to an hour) on a pathway tunnelled through the solid rock, for a marvellous view of the coastline. ☎ 96 597 2015 🕐 08.00–19.00 Mon–Fri, 08.00–16.00 Sat–Sun summer; 08.00–18.00 Mon–Fri, 09.00–15.00 Sat–Sun winter

TAKING A BREAK

La Cambra ££ This Spanish tavern of old with its cool interior of tiles and dark wood has a menu dominated by traditional rice dishes and featuring some tasty meat and seafood options such as pigeon, hake and locally caught prawns. ➌ Calle Delfín ☎ 96 583 0605 🕐 10.30–16.00 & 19.30–24.00

Los Zapatos £££ One of Calpe's oldest established restaurants, serving international haute cuisine. A gourmet heaven of superb food and fine wines. ➌ Calle Santa María 7 ☎ 96 583 1507 🕐 evenings 19.00–23.30, lunch 12.30–15.00, closed Tues–Wed ℹ️ Be sure to reserve a table well in advance. Wheelchair friendly

SHOPPING
Calpe's weekly market takes place on a Saturday on the northern outskirts of the Old Town.

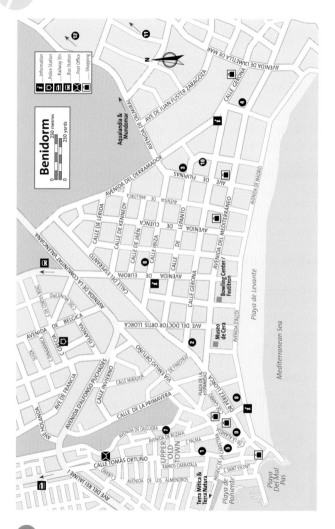

Benidorm

0 — 250 metres
0 — 250 yards

Information
Police Station
Railway Stn
Bus Station
Post Office
Shopping

N

Aqualandia & Mundomar

AVENIDA DE L'AMETLLA DE MAR
AVE DE JUAN FUSTER ZARAGOZA
AVENIDA DE L'AMIRAL
CALLE GERONA
AVENIDA DEL DERRAMADOR
AVE DE FILIPINAS
AVENIDA DE MALLORCA
AVENIDA DE MADRID
CALLE DE LERIDA
CALLE DE KENNEDY
AVENIDA DE CUENCA
AVENIDA DE LEPANTO
CALLE DEL ESPERANTO
CALLE DE JAÉN
CALLE DE IBIZA
CALLE DE EUROPA
AVENIDA DE LA COMUNITAT VALENCIANA
AVENIDA DEL MEDITERRANEO
CALLE GERONA
AVE DEL DOCTOR ORTIS LLORCA
Bowling Center / Festitron
Museo de Cera
AVENIDA D'ALCOI
Playa de Levante
Mediterranean Sea
C DE CORTES ROSE
CALLE MUNICIPIO
AVENIDA DE BELGICA
C GRANDIA
GRECIA
SUIZA
AVENIDA CARRATALA
AVE DE FRANCIA
AVENIDA D'ALFONSO PUCHADES
CALLE INVIERNO
CALLE MIRADOR
VIA EMILIO ORTUÑO
VIA DE FINESTRAT
CALLE DE LA PRIMAVERA
AVE HOLANDA
AVE DEL REI JAUME I
CALLE TOMÁS ORTUÑO
C URANO
AVENIDA DE L'AIGUERA
AVENIDA DE RUZAFA
C PALMA
UPPER OLD TOWN
RAMOS CARRATALA
AVENIDA DE LOS ALMENDROS
PASSEIG DE LA CARRATALA
C DE L'ALMETRA
C DE GABIO
DE PEREZ LLORCA
PLAZA DE LA HISPANIDAD
C SANT VICENT
Terra Mitica & Terra Natura
Playa de Poniente
Playa Del Mal Pas

Benidorm

Benidorm's beautiful bay is split into two sandy crescents by a rock promontory, once the site of a commanding **castle**. It is now topped by a tiled *mirador* (viewpoint), which provides panoramic views from its Mediterranean balcony. The Old Town of narrow streets behind the castle is the Spanish part of Benidorm, though there is no shortage of pubs and cafés run by expat *ingleses*.

BEACHES

Benidorm's twin beaches add up to 5 km (3 miles) of fine golden sand. Most of the action takes place along the east beach, the **Playa de Levante**. The long, pedestrianised promenade (beware local traffic) stretches east from the Old Town to the foothills of the Sierra Helada at Rincón de Loix, and is lined with restaurants and cafés, some with afternoon tea dances and evening entertainment. Look out for the beach sand sculptures, and go there on Sundays to see the locals dressed up for their traditional pre-lunch stroll (*paseo*). It is also pleasant for an evening amble, since the noisy discos have all been moved into another area of the town.

The west beach, **Playa de Poniente**, is longer and less crowded, and its shoreline is rock free. Here you will find a bit more privacy. It is backed by the Parque de Elche, whose breezy palms come from the town of the same name. Between the two, sheltered by the port and the cliffs of the castle, is the small beach of Mal Pas, where smugglers used to land their cargo. Most of the nautical activities take place here.

You can hire sunbeds and parasols for the day – hang on to your receipt so that you can prove you have paid, if asked. There are pedalos for hire at regular intervals along both beaches, which also have children's play areas, volleyball nets and diving platforms.

Take a souvenir snap of Gran Hotel Bali in La Cala (see page 110) – the tallest hotel in Europe and the tallest building in Spain (210 m/610 ft).

RESORTS

THINGS TO SEE & DO

Aqualandia
This thrilling water park – said to be the largest in Europe – certainly makes a big splash with visitors (see page 102).

ⓐ Sierra Helada, Rincón de Loix, Benidorm ⓣ 96 586 4006/7/8
ⓦ www.aqualandia.net ⓛ From 10.00 mid-May–mid-Oct ⓘ Admission charge

Ozone Bowling Center
Recreation centre with 10-pin bowling, ping-pong, billiards and other games.

ⓐ Avenida del Mediterráneo 22, next to Festitron ⓣ 96 585 4187
ⓛ 10.00–02.00 ⓘ Fee per game plus shoe hire

Festitron
Games arcade for big boys and girls, with large-screen Harley Riders and the like.

ⓐ Avenida del Mediterráneo next to Festilandia Park ⓛ 10.30–late
ⓘ Free entrance, pay per game

Mundomar
Next door to Aqualandia, the Costa Blanca's 'Seaworld' also has a colourful array of toucans, flamingoes, bats and birds. Dolphins perform twice a day in the dolphinarium, and the parrots and sea lions also put on a show (see page 103).

ⓐ Sierra Helada, Rincón de Loix, Benidorm ⓣ 96 586 9101/2/3
ⓦ www.mundomar.es ⓛ 10.00–19.00

Museo de Cera (Wax Museum)
Meet Elvis, Dracula and a host of other familiar faces at Benidorm's wax museum. Dads may also enjoy the Old Lead Soldiers Museum, with more than 2,000 figures from many conflicts and countries.

ⓐ Avenida del Mediterráneo 8 ⓣ 96 680 8421 ⓛ 11.00–01.00 summer; 10.00–21.00 winter ⓘ Admission charge

SHOPPING

The shops along Avenida del Mediterráneo, and those around or near Triangular Square in the old quarter, have several leather shops and the small shopping bazaars sell cheap T-shirts, beachwear and sun-dresses.

Arte Estudio Lucas A tiny old-town studio-shop. The artist specialises in painting coats of arms, and sells pretty paintings of the sea. ⓐ Calle del Mal Pas, opposite the church ⓘ 96 585 8914 ⓛ 09.30–13.00 & 18.00–21.00

Bodega El Barril Good range of booze at competitive prices. ⓐ Avenida del Mediterráneo 37 ⓘ 96 585 9018 ⓛ 09.30–20.00; closed Sun

Bordados Rodríguez Beautiful embroidered tablecloths, serviettes and other top quality goods. ⓐ Avenida Martínez Alejos 5, in the Old Town ⓛ 10.00–21.30 Mon–Sat

Carrefour A hypermarket. Bus no 12 runs from Rincón de Loix hourly (09.30–12.30 & 16.30–19.30). ⓐ Off the Benidorm bypass ⓛ 09.00–22.00 Mon–Sat

Casa de Cinturón Good-quality leather goods. ⓐ Avenida del Mediterráneo 18 ⓘ 96 585 0144 ⓛ 10.00–21.30 Mon–Sat

Douglas Fragrant shop selling cosmetics, perfumes and every brand and strength of sun block you can imagine – vital in these parts. ⓐ Calle Martinez Alejos 10 ⓛ 10.00–21.30

La Marina Shopping Centre Free basement parking plus three floors of fashion, electrical goods, jewellers, lingerie, opticians and cameras. The third floor features terraced restaurants, bars and a nine-screen cinema. ⓐ Behind Carrefour hypermarket on La Marina Commercial Estate ⓛ 09.00–22.00

Mercado Indoor market with stalls selling fresh fruit, vegetables, fish, meat and baked goods, as well as some clothes and souvenirs. ⓐ Avenida L'Ametlla de Mar ⓛ 08.30–15.00 Mon–Sat & 17.00–21.00 closed Sun

Mercadona Supermarket. ⓐ Avenida Alfonso Puchades (served by buses no 1 and no 8) ⓛ 10.00–20.30 Mon–Sat

◓ *Terra Mitica*

Sightseeing trains

Mini-trains depart outside the funfairs for a 25-minute ride around the Levante Beach.

🕐 Until late ❶ Admission charge

Terra Mítica

Over a million square metres of theme park based on the ancient civilisations of Egypt, Iberia, Rome, Greece and the Barbary Coast. The huge complex and its great stone constructions, including the Acropolis, the Colosseum and the Land of the Pharaohs, also features top-class themed restaurants and rides such as Colossus (the largest wooden roller coaster in Europe), the Cataracts of the Nile Tizona and the newly opened Inferno and Infinito (an observation tower). Miniature versions of all rides are available for young children.

ⓐ Just outside Benidorm (park has its own bus and train service)

❶ 90 202 0220 Ⓦ www.terramiticapark.com 🕐 10.00–20.00 (June–mid-Sept); until 24.00 (mid-July–early Sept); varying days 10.00–20.00 (mid-March–June and mid-Sept–Oct); closed (Nov–mid-March)

❶ €34 adults, €25.50 children aged 5–10, children aged 4 and under free; discounts for groups and senior citizens; a two-day ticket covers it all

Terra Natura

Embark on an adventure that takes the whole family around the world to see people and animals in their native settings and natural habitats. Education and fun rolled into one for kiddies and adults alike.

ⓐ Foia del Verdader 1 (next to Terra Mítica) ☎ 90 252 2333
ⓦ www.terranatura.com ⏰ 10.00–dusk ❶ Admission charge

Watersports

During high season the **Cable-Ski** operates at the Rincón de Loix end of Playa Levante (☎ 96 585 1386). Or hire a boat from **Carlos Launch Rental** at the port (☎ 96 585 3018).

TOURS
Calpe boat trip

For the best views of the coastline, take a boat ride from Benidorm to Calpe (see page 21). There is time to wander around the port beneath the majestic Peñón de Ifach before your return journey. Boat trips operate in summer only. Contact the tourist office for further details.

Isla de Benidorm (Peacock Island)

Visit that mysterious rock looming offshore, popularly known as Peacock Island because of the aviary there. The ten-minute boat ride from the port provides you with splendid views of Benidorm's skyline. The waters around the island are a marine reserve, and you can journey beneath the waves in the Aquascope for a mesmerising look at the schools of fish and colourful underwater life. Afterwards you can visit the bar or the peacock aviary, or hike the island trails. Boats return to Benidorm roughly every hour.

The Lemon Express

A trip from Benidorm to Gata de Gorgos on this jolly green train is the Costa Blanca's most popular tour, named after the lemon groves that once stretched to Altea. The single-track train reveals stunning coastal scenery as it winds its way through tunnels and along narrow ravines high above the sparkling sea, until it reaches Gata (see page 63), where you will have a quick tour of one of Spain's most popular guitar factories. Gata is known for its basketry and wickerwork, and there is time to visit shops selling these local handicrafts. A rollicking ride home is enhanced by free-flowing Lemon Express *cava* (sparkling wine). Ask for details at your hotel or book directly. ⓐ The train leaves from Benidorm station ⓣ 96 680 3103 ⓛ Runs Tues–Sat

EXCURSION
Cuevas de Canalobre

Unlike many caves, which are the geological equivalent of damp dungeons, at 70 m (230 ft) high, this ornate cavern has one of the highest vaults in Spain, with a year-round constant temperature of 18°C (64°F). Estimated to be around seven million years old, this collection of weirdly shaped stalagmites and stalactites was discovered in the 8th century by the Moors; more recently it was used as a secret aircraft engine factory during the Civil War. There is a guided tour set to a background of classical music, which gives it a cathedral-like feel – the acoustics are so good.

⬥ *The beach at Benidorm*

🅐 Busot, 24 km (15 miles) east of Alicante, 40 km (25 miles) west of Benidorm ☎ 96 569 9250 🕐 10.30–19.50 Easter and mid-June–Sept; 11.00–17.50 Oct–early June; guided tours every 30–40 minutes; concerts often take place here Mar–Apr and Nov–Dec ❗ Admission charge

The Cuevas de Canalobre is a popular tourist destination, so it is a good idea to go later in the day if you want to visit in smaller groups. You could stop off on the way back for dinner at the family-run Mesón Restaurante 5 Hermanos. It specialises in paella, chargrilled meats and *conejo al ajillo* (garlic rabbit). 🅐 on the road towards Busot ☎ 96 569 9102

TAKING A BREAK

Cervecería Gambrinus £ ❶ Few venture into Benidorm's old town to drink, but this very Spanish, noisy, bustling temple to the hop is worth seeking out for its tapas and frothy tankards, served at the long wooden bar. 🅐 Calle Tomás Ortuño 10 🕐 08.00–02.00

India Gate £ ❷ A long-established Tandoori restaurant with a large selection of curries from all over the subcontinent, a menu in English and a bone fide Indian chef. 🅐 Calle Gerona 2/14 ☎ 63 605 9785 🌐 www.restaurantindiagate.com 🕐 18.00–late

Joker's £ ❸ Alcohol by the pitcher, greasy plates of English stodge, big screen TV showing English footy, free shots, kinky late-night shows – in short, the full-on Benidorm experience. 🅐 Avenida de Filipinas 🕐 20.00–08.00

Cactus Cantina £–££ ❹ Fill up on steaks, tortillas, omelettes, fish and chilli con carne at this brightly decorated Mexican-Californian eatery which, tongue in cheek, claims to have been around since 1492. 🅐 Avenida del Mediterráneo 51 ☎ 96 683 1616 🕐 12.00–late

La Cava Aragonesa ££ ❺ Pleasant bar with possibly the best tapas in town. Dishes are displayed in a glass counter, below the hanging hams. Champagne and wines. ⓐ Plaza de la Constitución 2, Old Town ❶ 96 680 1206 ❷ 12.00–01.00

El Tapeo Andaluz ££ ❻ This authentic Spanish eatery is a whirl of frenetic activity at lunchtime, with an excellent *menú del día* and plenty of traditional dishes. ⓐ Calle de Ibiza 12 ❶ 96 680 6899 ❷ 08.00–23.00

Aitona ££–£££ ❼ Look for the giant prawn and paella pan advertising this fish restaurant, which also serves meats and paellas. ⓐ Calle Ruzafa, Old Town ❶ 96 585 3010 ❷ 13.00–16.00 & 20.00–23.30

AFTER DARK

The Levante side has the liveliest entertainment, with a variety of disco pubs and cabaret bars along Avenida del Mediterráneo and Calle Ibiza. Many singers and comedians come from the UK's northern club circuit.

The disco pubs attract a young international set. The main focus is on a pedestrianised walkway, known as the 'square', where Avenida de Mallorca intersects Calle Gerona. Some bars on the Levante beach feature bands playing Spanish music. Entry is usually free but drinks may be more pricey. In the Old Town, Calle Sant Vicent is one of several narrow streets lined with small pubs.

Penelope Beach Club ££ ❽ One of Benidorm's most famous nightclubs offers two locations for dancing the night away. Penelope Beach Club is right on the waterfront along Av. de la Mare de Déu del Sofratge by Playa de Levante, with a cocktail bar and late-night disco. Or head for the mega-club Penelope Discoteca with top DJs and dancers on the disco strip, Carretera Alicante-Valencia km 122. ❷ 23.00–06.00 summer

Rich Bitch ££ ❾ Drag and comedy featuring Jordan Rivers and company. Show starts at 22.30, but you must book in advance and take your seat by 21.30 or you will lose it to the queues outside. Expect to pay a small cover charge. Rich Bitch memorabilia is on sale and is also offered as raffle prizes. Cameras allowed but no camcorders. ⓐ Calle de Pal 4, Benidorm Old Town ⓣ 96 605 5906 ⓛ 21.00–01.00

Top of the Pops ££ ❿ Well-known disco pub, recently renovated, playing up-to-the-minute sounds. ⓐ Avenida Almería 5 ⓛ 21.00 to the early hours ⓘ 'Anything goes' dress code

◉ View over Benidorm

● *Follow a buzzing night of clubbing with a relaxing day on the beach*

It is wise to ignore the touts who approach you at bars or on the street or beach selling cheap 'gold' chains – they are nothing but fool's gold.

Benidorm Palace £££ ⓫   This big, gorgeous, three-hour floorshow is the highlight of Costa Blanca entertainment, featuring glittering Las Vegas-style cabaret acts, Spanish dancers and flamenco, horses, jugglers and magicians. ⓐ Av. del Doctor Severo Ochoa 13 ❶ 96 585 1660/61 🕒 Doors open at 21.00, shows run 22.00–01.30. Show days vary ❶ There are tour coaches from Benidorm hotels and several other resorts; admission is good value and includes the first drink; dinner (optional) is also served.

Castle Conde de Alfaz £££ ⓬   Feasting and merrymaking, medieval-style, for all ages. Armoured knights on horseback joust and duel before the king and queen. Sing along with court jesters, or descend into the Pit of Terror. ⓐ In Alfaz between Altea and Benidorm ❶ 96 686 5592/3 🕒 Doors open 20.00; show days vary year-round

La Cala de Finestrat

La Cala de Finestrat is a large, sandy cove on the southern outskirts of Benidorm, part of the municipality of Finestrat, which includes the ancient village in the foothills of the Puig Campana mountain 8 km (5 miles) inland. The beach area with its promenades is on a smaller scale than the larger and noisier Benidorm beaches and is highly favoured by the Spanish locals. A large car park provides free all-day parking.

The village of Finestrat (population 950) dates from the Iberian era and was the local centre of olive farming during the Moorish occupation. Olive and almond trees still abound, flowering in early spring to cover the hills in a show of pink and white blossoms. Its narrow streets and multicoloured houses, climbing to the lookout point of La Hermita, make it one of the most visited villages on the Costa Blanca. Of interest are the 18th-century blue-domed church with its ceiling and wall frescoes and the nearby fountains of Font de Molí. For the best local produce, try the **fruit and vegetable markets** held in Finestrat village and La Cala de Finestrat on Fridays. ● Both open around 09.00–14.00

⏷ Finestrat village is south of Benidorm

BEACHES

La Cala de Finestrat is one of the best beaches on the Costa Blanca, a fine sweep of sheltered sand, with a promenade lined by shops, cafés and restaurants. Sunbeds and sunshades are for hire, as well as pedalos.

If you are in Finestrat during August, join the St Bartholomew festivities. From 22 to 25 August, the village throngs with crowds enjoying good local food and wine, as well as processions and fireworks.

TAKING A BREAK

El Arenal £–££ Perennially popular for its seafood paella, this Spanish restaurant on the seafront has a shaded terrace on which to enjoy a leisurely meal. 🄰 Avenida Marina Baixa, La Cala Finestrat 🄱 96 585 6700 🄲 13.00–16.00 & 20.00–23.00 summer; 13.00–16.00 winter

La Morena ££ An exquisite, family-run restaurant set amid almond and olive groves, with excellent cuisine. Specialises in fresh fish, *cabrito* (kid) and tender young lamb. Large range of local and national wines. 🄰 Carretera Benidorm, 8 km (5 miles) inland, outside Finestrat village 🄱 96 587 8539 🄲 13.00–16.00 & 20.00–23.30 Tues–Sat; closed Mon 🄳 Reservations recommended

El Pescador ££ This restaurant has stunning sea views and is popular for lunch. Specialises in fresh local fish and is famous for its hundreds of varieties of traditional local rice dishes. Very good steaks. 🄰 At the far end of La Cala beach 🄲 Lunch and dinner

AFTER DARK

Bounders A lively English-style pub, with karaoke every night and major sporting events shown on satellite TV. As well as the excellent bar snacks, try the popular Sunday lunch. 🄰 Avenida Marina Baixa, La Cala Finestrat 🄲 21.00–late

Villajoyosa

Villajoyosa, capital of the Marina Baixa district, has two distinct areas – a quaint old village and a modern industrial centre. Like many of the towns along the coast, Villajoyosa depends partly on fishing for its income – each day's catch is auctioned off in the late afternoon at the port.

The narrow streets of the old quarter have real character, with rainbow-coloured houses fanning out from the Church of Our Lady of the Assumption and along the seafront. The façades are deliberately painted in bright colours so that they are visible to sailors out at sea. It is a lovely area to wander around – stop for lunch at one of the many restaurants around Plaza San Pedro.

◔ *Coloured houses on Villajoyosa waterfront*

The tourist office in Villajoyosa is at the top of the Old Town, just off the main road. ⓐ Avenida País Valenciá 10 ⓣ 96 685 1371

BEACHES

Villajoyosa has 3.5 km (2 miles) of relatively uncrowded beaches. The longest and most central is the Blue Flag Playa Centro, which has fine, pale sand and runs from the old quarter up to the port. Nudists favour the isolated Playa del Racó Conill, 3 km (2 miles) out of town towards Benidorm.

Villajoyosa is famous for its chocolate-making industry – be sure to try some while you are here.

THINGS TO SEE & DO

Fiestas

Villajoyosa's Moors and Christians fiesta, in the last week of July, turns the streets into a parade ground of marching bands and colourful costumes.

TAKING A BREAK

Hogar del Pescador ££ The tiled and whitewashed dining room of this eatery, one street back from the beach, is one of the best places in town to try some local seafood paella, Mediterranean prawns and a whole host of locally caught fish. ⓐ Avenida País Valenciá 33 ⓣ 96 589 0021 ⓛ 12.00–16.00 & 19.30–24.00

SHOPPING
Villajoyosa's weekly market takes place on Thursday mornings on the northern side of town.

Santa Pola

Famous as a fishing port since Roman times, Santa Pola is now popular with holidaymakers for its beautiful sandy beaches. They do not suffer from the chock-a-block feel of some of the bigger resorts and are protected from easterly winds by the lighthouse-topped cape, 3 km (2 miles) northeast of town.

BEACHES

The long, sandy beaches to the west (Playa Libre, Tamarit – a Blue Flag beach – Playa Lissa and Gran Playa) are particularly suitable for children because the water is shallow for a long way out. East of Santa Pola are two more Blue Flag beaches – the central Playa Levante, and Playa Varadero on the eastern edge of the town.

THINGS TO SEE & DO

Aquarium

This small aquarium offers a good window on the Mediterranean, with close-ups of the ferocious-looking sea snakes, the graceful sea turtle and the Med's only tropical fish, the glamorous blue, gold and orange *pez verde*.

🅐 Plaza Fco, Fernández Ordóñez 🅣 96 541 6916 🅛 11.00–13.00 & 18.00–22.00 Tues–Sat, 10.00–13.00 Sun summer; 10.00–13.00 & 17.00–19.00 Tue–Sat, 10.00–13.00 Sun winter 🅘 Admission charge

Castle and Maritime Museum

The impressive 16th-century castle houses a museum that pays homage to the role of the sea in the life of Santa Pola.

🅐 Plaza del Castillo 🅣 96 669 1532 🅛 11.00–13.00 & 18.00–22.00 Tues–Sat, 11.00–13.30 Sun summer; 11.00–13.00 & 16.00–19.00 Tues–Sat, 11.00–13.30 Sun winter 🅘 Admission charge

● *The castle at Santa Pola*

SHOPPING
Santa Pola's local market takes place on Monday and Saturday mornings off Plaza de la Diputación.

Isla de Tabarca

This car-free island is a pleasant half-hour boat ride from Santa Pola. Once a pirates' stronghold, Tabarca is now a marine reserve, which makes it a top spot for snorkelling. The island is only 2 km (1¼ miles) long and around 400 m (435 yds) wide, so you can walk right around it, wander through the walled village or sample the local speciality of *caldero*, a rice dish made with fish stock, cooked in an iron pot. In high season boats run roughly every half hour (🕒 09.30–19.30) from Santa Pola's port, and much less frequently in winter (📞 96 541 1113 for times).

Pola Park

Children will love Pola Park, a large amusement park complete with bumper cars, roller coasters and all manner of stomach-churning fairground rides.

ⓐ Avenida Zaragoza 🕒 19.30–02.00 summer; weekends only 18.00–12.00 winter ❶ Free entry, pay per ride

Salt flats

Take a drive south towards Cartagena past the *salinas*, salt flats that yield up the huge white mountains adorning the grounds of the nearby salt refineries. The lakes are home to a large population of flamingos.

TAKING A BREAK

Restaurante Polamar ££ This lively beachside bar serves a good selection of tapas and sandwiches on a huge, sunny terrace. The cool, upmarket restaurant inside the adjoining hotel specialises in fish dishes.
ⓐ Playa de Levante 📞 96 541 3200

Gelatería Miami ££–£££ Delicious ice creams, waffles and freshly made crêpes with every topping under the sun are served up at shady outdoor tables. ⓐ Calle del Muelle

Guardamar del Segura

Topped by the ruins of a 13th-century castle, the small town of
Guardamar del Segura, which was formerly a fishing village, is
surrounded by scenic beaches and sand dunes. The sand dunes
themselves were planted with pines, palms and eucalyptus trees
at the beginning of the 20th century to stop the moving sand from
swallowing up the town.

BEACHES

Guardamar del Segura has five long, sandy beaches. The two nearest to
the town centre, La Roqueta and Playa Centro, have all the usual facilities
– umbrellas, sun-loungers and pedalos.

However, if you fancy escaping from all of the high-season holidaymakers for an hour or two, head north to Playa Vivers. The pretty beach
here is uncommercialised and uncrowded, lined by a row of quaint
fishermen's cottages. The beach is backed by the Dunas de Guardamar,
a beautiful, shady forest of pines and palms that is perfect for picnics.

TAKING A BREAK

Beach Bar Casablanca ££ Situated just beyond Playa Roqueta,
overlooking the beach, this efficient restaurant serves something for
everyone, from full-blown meat and fish dishes to omelettes, pasta
and paella and a large choice of salads and burgers. ⓐ Avenida Perú 2
ⓘ 96 672 5822

February is the month of the lively and colourful *carnaval* in Guardamar
del Segura – Easter Week sees a host of ceremonial and religious
processions, the Moors and Christians make their appearance in the last
two weeks of July, and 7 October is a fiesta for the town's patron saint,
the Virgen del Rosario.

La Manga & Mar Menor

Mar Menor (literally 'the minor sea') is separated from the Mediterranean by a thin strip of land about 21 km (13 miles) long, known as La Manga. This has the effect of turning Mar Menor into a huge swimming pool with warm, calm waters – the water temperature rarely drops below 18°C (64°F), even in winter. This is where people come to play: there are all kinds of watersports on offer, from sailing to diving and windsurfing, as well as huge stretches of fine white sand for dedicated sun worshippers.

As you are driving around this area, make sure you look out for windmills – some are in a sorry state, but others have been restored to their former glory.

BEACHES

If you are in search of solitude, Calblanque, a few kilometres before La Manga, is the place to head for. A very rough 5-km (3-mile) track keeps all but the most determined peace seekers away, but the long stretch of near-empty terracotta sand backed by rocky cliffs (no facilities) is worth the tortuous drive. There are white sandy beaches all along La Manga. On the mainland side, the Blue Flag beach of Santiago de la Ribera has good facilities.

The high concentration of salt and iodine in Mar Menor is said to be highly beneficial to anyone suffering from skin complaints.

THINGS TO SEE & DO

Bike riding and walking

The tourist office at the beginning of La Manga (☎ 96 814 6136) has a brochure of cycling and walking itineraries (look for a blue and white building near a sloping tower topped by a sphere).

● *Cabo de Palos beach in the Calblanque National Park*

Diving
The area around the lighthouse, Cabo de Palos, is renowned for its excellent diving. There are several diving schools nearby, including the **Club Islas Hormigas**. ⓐ Los Belones ❶ 96 817 5000, ext 1360

Golf
Golf at La Manga Club: Internationally famous for its three championship golf courses, this exclusive sport and leisure resort also offers horse riding, tennis, squash and bowls. ❶ 96 833 1234

Sailing and windsurfing
Manga Surf: This friendly school with English-speaking instructors offers private windsurfing and sailing lessons at affordable prices. If you already know what you are doing, you can just hire the boards or catamarans, or opt for a less technical paddle about in a canoe or pedalo. ⓐ Gran Vía, exit 23 ❶ 96 814 5331 ● 09.00–21.00

● *Denia castle offers a wonderful view of the sea and the town*

EXCURSIONS
Out & about

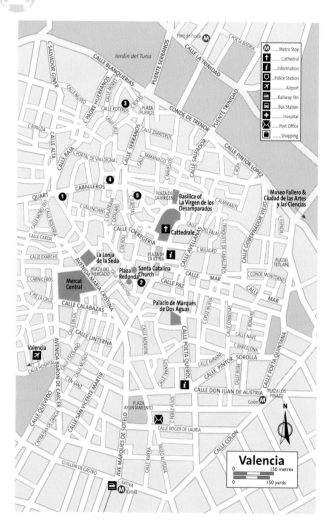

Valencia

Ⓜ	Metro Stop
✝	Cathedral
ℹ	Information
	Police Station
	Airport
	Railway Stn
	Bus Station
✚	Hospital
✉	Post Office
🛍	Shopping

C SALVADOR GINER
CALLE BLANQUERIAS
Jardin del Turia
PUENTE SERRANOS
CALLE LA TRINIDAD
C POETA BODRIA
Pont de Fusta Ⓜ
C PADRE HUERFANOS
CALLE MUSEO
CALLE MONT
CALLE NOBET
PLAZA FUEROS
CALLE ROTEROS
ZURRADORES
CONDE DE TRENOR
PUENTE TRINIDAD
C RIPALDA
CALLE ALTA
CALLE BAJA
PORTAL DE VALLDIGNA
CALLE SERRANOS
CALLE ZAPATEROS
CALLE SAMANIEGO
CAVELLOS
CALLE SALVADOR
CALLE PINTOR LOPEZ
C BOIX
CABALLEROS
QUART
CALLE MOSSEN FEBRER
CALLE BOSSERIA
CALLE VALENCIANS
CUATRETE
EN BOU
CALLE CORREGERIA
PLAZA DE LA VIRGEN
Basílica of La Virgen de los Desamparados
ALMIRANTE
CALLE DEL PALAU
CHENOUET DE CABALLERS
CALLE GOBERNADOR VIEJO
ESPARA
Museo Fallero & Ciudad de las Artes y las Ciencias
CALLE CARDA
CALLE EXARCHS
C CARNICEROS
C PIE LA CRUZ
AVENIDA MARIA CRISTINA
✝ Cattedrale
CALLE AVELLANAS
C MILAGRO
PLAZA TETUAN
PLAZA DE LA REINA
ℹ
La Lonja de la Seda
PLAZA DEL MERCADO
Santa Catalina Church
Plaza Redonda
CALLE PAZ
CALLE MAR
C CONDE MONTORNES
Mercat Central
CALLE CALABAZAS
Palacio de Marqués de Dos Aguas
CRUZ NUEVA
CALLE COMEDIAS
CALLE MAR
CALLE LINTERNA
CALLE MORATIN
CALLE POETA QUEROL
CALLE NAVE
C BONAIRE
Valencia ✈
AVENIDA BARON DE CARCER
CALLE MUSEO
CALLE ESCOLANO
C EN SANZ
CALLE PINTOR
SOROLLA
C BARCELONA
CALLE BIBE
CALLE POETA QUINTANA
CALLE HOSPITAL
CALLE QUEVEDO
C ENTRASAR DE GRACIA
CALLE SAN VICENTE MARTIR
CALLE TRANSITS
ℹ
CALLE DON JUAN DE AUSTRIA
PLAZA LOS PINAZO
Colón Ⓜ
PLAZA AYUNTAMIENTO
✉
C PEREZ PUJOL
CALLE ROGER DE LAURIA
N
GUILLEM DE CASTRO
AVE MARQUES DE SOTELO
CALLE RIBERA
CALLE COLON
Valencia
0   150 metres
0   150 yards
🛍 Ⓜ
Xativa

Valencia

Valencia, founded by the Romans, became one of the biggest and richest cities in medieval Spain, thanks to its fine harbour. Today it is the country's third-largest city and a regional capital, with many monuments and museums.

Valencia can be visited on a tour from resorts on the Costa Blanca, or independently by bus or car. Along the way you will see terraced fields of

◆ *Valencia Cathedral, Plaza de la Reina*

olive and almond trees, rice fields and the orange and lemon groves for which the province is known. Tours normally stop en route at the Lladró factory outlet store and take you to the cathedral, the Fallas Museum and El Corte Inglés, Spain's largest chain of department stores.

THINGS TO SEE & DO

Valencia is huge, and you will not be able to cover all of its monuments and sights on one tour. Those listed in this first section are the ones normally visited on an organised tour. The second section (Exploring on Your Own, see page 51) contains suggestions for worthwhile visits to other attractions if you are making your own way. You will need a good map if you want to explore on your own, which you can obtain from one of the tourist offices.

🔺 *Shopping at the stylish Mercat Central*

Valencia tourist offices are open 10.00–18.30 Mon–Sat
ⓐ Plaza de la Reina 19 ❶ 06 315 3931 ⓐ Calle Paz 48 ❶ 96 398 6422
ⓐ At the train station, Estación del Norte, Játiva 24 ❶ 96 352 8573
ⓐ Calle Poeta Querol ❶ 96 351 4907 ⓦ www.turisvalencia.es

La Cattedrale (The Cathedral)

Built on the site of an Arab mosque, Valencia's cathedral took 350 years
to construct and reflects Romanesque, Gothic, baroque and Renaissance
styles. It claims to possess the Holy Grail, said to have been brought here
from Jerusalem in the 13th century. The alabaster stone cup is encased
in glass in the Capilla del Santo Caliz. Alongside is the cathedral
museum. You can also climb the steps to the top of the bell tower, the
Miguelete Tower, for a view over the city.
ⓐ Plaza de la Reina ⏰ **Cathedral** 10.00–18.00 Mon–Fri, until 17.30 Sat,
until 14.00 Sun; **Miguelete Tower** 10.30–12.30 & 16.30–19.00 (until 18.00
in winter) ❶ Cathedral museum, admission charge

Near the Cathedral

Behind the cathedral in the Plaza de la Virgen is the smaller **Basilica of
La Virgen de los Desamparados** (Our Lady of the Forsaken), dedicated
to the protector of Valencia. ⏰ 07.00–14.00 & 16.00–21.00

Return to the Plaza de la Reina (the coach drop-off point) and turn
right at the *croissanteria* for a closer look at the soaring tower of Santa
Catalina church. A bit further on is Plaza Lope de Vega, where, off a side
alley, you will find the little **Plaza Redonda**, a circle of old, tiled market
stalls selling fabrics and ceramics around a fountain. ⏰ Closed Sun

Carry on to the busy **Plaza del Mercado** and turn right to reach **La
Lonja de la Seda**, the Old Silk Exchange. This huge 15th-century Gothic
building is classified as a UNESCO World Heritage Site, and is now used
for exhibitions. ⏰ Closed Mon, and Sun afternoon

Opposite is the **Mercat Central** (Central Market), with its modernist-
style façade, tiled dome and stained glass windows. This is the place to
come to buy olives as big as plums, huge chunks of watermelon and
giant, sun-kissed peaches. ⏰ Mon–Sat

Museo Fallero (Fallas Museum)

Artists work year round to create giant satirical papier mâché figures, which are paraded through the streets and burned on the last night of Valencia's main festival, the *fallas*. This humorous museum houses a collection of some of these, dating from 1934 to the present day. Offerings include Indiana Jones, Yoda and Jacques Cousteau as well as Samurai tourists and wrinkled, picnicking pensioners.

🅐 Plaza Monteolivete ☎ 96 352 5478 🕐 10.00–14.00 & 16.30–20.00 Tues–Sat, 10.00–15.00 Sun ❶ Admission charge

Museo Fallero is a 30- to 40-minute walk from the town centre, so it is worth taking a taxi, which will not cost more than the price of a drink and a sandwich. From the museum, the City of Art and Science (see opposite) is about a ten-minute walk away.

SHOPPING

El Corte Inglés This branch of Spain's biggest department store chain is near the tourist office, about a ten-minute walk from Plaza de la Reina. The main entrance (and coach stop) is along Calle Pintor Sorolla. There are restaurants on the top floor and toilets on the second floor.

Lladró Spain's only handmade porcelain factory is world famous. Excursions visit the factory showroom in a town northwest of Valencia (you cannot tour the workshop itself), which features hundreds of porcelain figures in all shapes and sizes. 'Seconds' are sold at discount prices. 🅐 Tabernes Blanque ☎ 96 185 1570 🕐 09.30–19.30 Mon–Fri, 09.30–13.30 Sat

Mercat Central See page 49.

El Rastro Valencia's largest market – everything from local handicrafts to clothes and food. 🅐 Mestalla, east of the river 🕐 Sundays

EXPLORING ON YOUR OWN

There is a daily coach service to Valencia from Benidorm that departs from the Ubesa office at Avenida Europa 8. It is best to buy your ticket and reserve your seat at the office the day before. Buses run roughly every two to three hours, at 08.00–21.40 hours. The journey takes just under two hours and leaves you at Valencia's bus station, where you should go upstairs to the ticket office and reserve your seat for the return journey. Bus no 8 from the front of the bus station will take you to Plaza de la Reina in the centre of town. Buy your ticket on the bus.

Ciudad de las Artes y las Ciencias (City of Art and Science)

Valencia's massive cultural, educational and leisure centre lies on the outskirts of the city centre. L'Hemisfèric, a hi-tech, shell-shaped building surrounded by water, alternates planetarium and laser shows with action-packed, documentary-style films on giant screens in the IMAX cinema (soundtracks available in English). This huge interactive science museum has now been joined by an oceanography park, complete with dolphinarium, and a performing arts and cultural centre.

ⓐ Arzobispo Mayoral 14 ⓣ 90 210 0031 ⓛ 10.00–21.00 summer; 10.00–19.00 winter ⓦ www.cac.es

Palacio de Marqués de Dos Aguas (National Ceramics Museum)

The elaborate baroque façade of this 18th-century building opens up on to an ornate mix of grandiose stately home decor and exquisite ceramics. A series of displays traces the history of this traditional Valencian craft from the 13th century onwards, including the famous Manises pottery. Do not miss the Salita de Porcelana with its porcelain-adorned chairs, the Dormitorio del Marqués with the elaborate four-poster bed and marble bath, and the Red Room, where glorious red upholstery contrasts with sea-green walls. There is also a room containing 18th-century carriages.

ⓐ Rinconada García Sanchis ⓣ 96 351 6392 ⓛ 10.00–14.00 & 16.00–20.00 Tues–Sat, 10.00–14.00 Sun ⓘ Admission charge

TAKING A BREAK

Café Sant Jaume £ ❶ This tiny, open-all-hours café, tucked away in the Barrio del Carmen district of the city centre, is worth seeking out for a relaxing drink or snack in the shade of tall trees on a pretty square, the friendly waiters and the old world charm of its carved wood interior. Popular with locals. ⓐ Calle de Caballeros 51 🕒 06.30–01.30

Horchateria de Santa Catalina £–££ ❷ A *horchateria* is where they produce and serve *horchata*, a sweet drink made with ground tigernuts, sugar and milk and this no-nonsense marble-and-tiles café is the best place in town to dunk a few *churros* (a thin doughnut) into a creamy glassful. Upstairs is a more formal restaurant with crystal chandeliers, tinkling glasses and a menu of paella and seafood. ⓐ Plaza de Santa Catalina 6 🕿 96 391 2379 🕒 Restaurant 13.00–16.00 & 20.00–23.00

El Forcat ££ ❸ The folksy dining room of the El Forcat is one of the best places in town to sample Valencia's famous paella. Traditional handicrafts bedeck almost every surface and only local Valencian rice is used in the dishes. ⓐ Calle Roteros 12 🕿 96 391 1213 🕒 13.30–16.00 & 20.30–24.00

Montealban ££ ❹ Whether you are just after a cheap and cheerful *menú del día* or full evening meal, this modern place in the heart of the historical core is a sound option. ⓐ Calle de Caballeros 10 🕿 96 392 4495 🕒 12.00–16.00 & 20.30–01.00

Restaurante Generalife £££ ❺ Welcoming restaurant offering some slightly unusual dishes such as chops with honey and steak with roquefort sauce, as well as regional rice specialities such as *arroz a banda* (rice with fish). ⓐ Calle de Caballeros 5 🕿 96 391 7899 🕒 13.30–15.30 & 20.30–23.30

Xàtiva

Xàtiva (pronounced 'Sha-tiva'), is the more usual name for the Castillian version, Jàtiva. It is situated 40 km (25 miles) inland, and is reached by a road that winds through a fertile valley of lemon and olive groves up towards the mountains. The Iberians, the Romans and the Carthaginians under Hannibal have all played a part in the history of this ancient town, the site of Europe's first paper mill, built by the Moors in 1150. Today, Xàtiva is well known for the many fountains that grace its squares, its attractive old quarter and a magnificent castle perched on the hill over-looking the red roofs of the town below.

Xàtiva is not very well signposted from the coast – follow signs for Albaida to begin with.

BEACHES

If you need to cool off after all that sightseeing, head to the clean, sandy beaches at the coastal town of Gandía (40 km/25 miles from Xàtiva).

THINGS TO SEE & DO

Almodí Museum

Housed in a beautiful Renaissance building, this spacious museum contains a variety of archaeological exhibits as well as a collection of predominantly 17th-century paintings by Spanish artists. There are several by José Ribera (El Españoleto) who was born in Xàtiva in 1591. Look out for the portrait of the Spanish king, Felipe V, which hangs upside down as a symbolic revenge on the monarch for ordering the burning of Xàtiva in 1707. Do not miss the lovely cloistered patio.
ⓐ Calle Corretgeria 46 ❶ 96 227 6597 ❷ 09.30–14.30 Tues–Fri summer; 10.00–14.00 & 16.00–18.00 Tues–Fri winter; 10.00–14.00 Sat–Sun year round ❶ Admission charge

The Castle

The imposing, well-preserved walls of Xàtiva's castle stretch along the crest of the hill overlooking the town. Although the ridge was fortified as far back as Iberian and Roman times, many of the surviving features date from the Moorish and Gothic eras. A series of impressive gates leads through the upper castle to a dark prison, a Gothic chapel in which several inmates are buried, and a series of watchtowers with great panoramas over Xàtiva and the surrounding valleys. The older, lower castle has a lovely view back over the main castle from the open balcony in the Queen's Tower, which was named after Himilce, Hannibal's wife, who gave birth to a son here in 218 BC.

ℹ 96 227 4274 🕐 10.00–19.00 Tues–Fri summer; 10.00–18.00 winter
❗ Admission charge

Children

If you are visiting with children, or just plain footsore, a little train leaves from the front of the tourist office to do the rounds of Xàtiva's sights.

🕐 12.30 & 17.30 Tues–Sat, 12.00, 13.00, 17.00 & 18.00 Sun

Iglesia de Sant Feliu

This 13th-century church is the oldest in Xàtiva, famed for its Roman columns, Spanish Renaissance paintings and outstanding architecture.

🕐 10.00–13.00 & 16.00–19.00 Mon–Sat, 10.00–13.00 Sun

Nits al Castell

The Nits al Castell (Nights at the Castle) programme puts on a series of evening performances of ballet, classical music, flamenco and jazz throughout July. Reservations can be made through the tourist office.

SHOPPING
Enjoy searching for bargains in the hustle and bustle of the charming marketplace on Tuesday and Friday mornings.

🅐 Albereda Jaume I 50 🕾 96 227 3346 🕒 10.00–14.30 & 17.00–19.00
Tues–Fri, 10.00–14.00 Sat & Sun

Walking tour of the Old Town
A good starting point for a walking tour of the Old Town is Portal Sant
Francesc, a square with a baroque fountain. From there, head along
the narrow Calle Montcada to the Gothic fountain in front of the
18th-century Palacio de Justicia. Here you can carry straight on past the
13th-century church (Iglesia de San Pedro) to the lovely fountain at the
end of the town, where locals queue up to fill all manner of receptacles
with the spring water gushing from its 25 spouts.

Alternatively, you can take Calle Sanchis to the impressive basilica
(La Seu), which was started in 1596, although the main façade was
finished in 1920 (🕒 For visits 10.30–13.00 Mon–Sat). Take a look at the
beautiful carving and pillars on the 15th-century hospital opposite.
A little further on, steps lead to the market place, an attractive arched
square fringed by crumbling façades and wrought-iron balconies.
You can end your tour at the Almodí Museum just beyond.

It is no surprise that Xàtiva has plenty of churches: two Borgia popes
– Calixtus III and Alexander VI – were born in the town in the 14th and
15th centuries.

TAKING A BREAK

There are several bars along the Albereda Jaume I that serve sandwiches
and snacks at outdoor tables.

La Forca ££ Locals meander in and out of this attractive tiled restaurant,
which specialises in regional cooking, to take away with them huge
dishes of paella. The *arroz caldoso*, rice with vegetables, rabbit and
chicken, are definitely worth trying, as is the excellent, homemade *flan*
(crème caramel). You can also pop in for tapas at the bar.
🅐 Calle Abad Pla 🕾 96 227 3402 🕒 For lunch Tues–Sun, for dinner
Fri–Sat

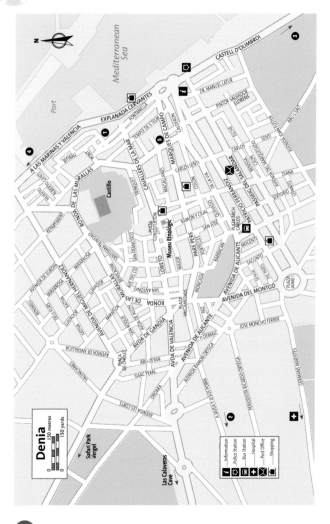

Denia

With beautiful beaches, a busy port, natural landscapes and an interesting old town to explore, Denia will keep you occupied for a good while. The castle looming overhead was built during the Islamic era (11th to 12th centuries) – it is a great place to escape from the afternoon heat.

The tourist office near the seafront (ⓐ Plaza Oculista Buigues 9 ❶ 96 642 2367) is very helpful. Ask for their map of the cultural route that takes you along the most picturesque streets. The old Baix de la Mar quarter opposite the port is particularly colourful.

Below the castle, the Town Hall and the Eglesia Asunción flank tiny Plaza de la Constitución. From here you can follow Calle Cop, a good shopping street, down to Plaza la Glorieta, a focal point for town festivities. The Marqués de Campo, with its tall canopy of leafy plane trees, leads down to the waterfront. In the evening, stalls selling bags, crafts and jewellery set up along Explanada Cervantes.

Do not follow the confusing signs to the tourist office – head for the Estación Marítima or, failing that, the port.

BEACHES

Denia has nearly 12 km (7½ miles) of coastline, with wide, sandy beaches and rocky coastal cliffs. There are long stretches of sandy beach to either side of the port. Sailing, windsurfing, diving and fishing are all on offer for watersports lovers.

If you are here in July, do not miss Bous a la Mar (Bulls at the Sea), part of Denia's Santísima Sangre fiesta. A bullring is set up along the seaside, and spectators watch the local boys enticing the bulls to chase them into the sea. The afternoon show is free.

THINGS TO SEE & DO

Las Calaveras Cave

Tall domes, stalactites and stalagmites mark the 300-m (984-ft) long passage through this prehistoric cave.

ⓐ 8 km (5 miles) from Gata de Gorgos on the road between Pedreguer and Benidoleig **ⓣ** 96 640 4235 **ⓘ** Admission charge

Castillo (The Castle)

It is a steep walk up to the castle, but you can take a train from the station opposite the tourist office. The castle has ruins from the Islamic and medieval periods. It was abandoned in 1859. Today, the enormous grounds seem like a large, shady park, with watchtowers and ramparts to explore and fantastic views over the town and waterfront.

SHOPPING

Denia's weekly market displays its wares on Monday mornings, with a small antiques market on Fridays, just around the corner from Plaza Jaime 1. Try also:

Bolsos Paco A good leather shop with reasonable prices.
ⓐ Calle Patricio Ferrandiz 27 **ⓣ** 96 642 1312

Marsal Shoes and exclusive leather goods plus fabulous swimming costumes, good-value cosmetics and perfumes, and upmarket knick-knacks. **ⓐ** Marqués de Campo 28
ⓒ Closed Sun

Mercadillo de Verano The 'summer market', opens daily in summer with stalls selling traditional handicrafts and modern art and crafts. **ⓐ** Esplanada de Cervantes **ⓒ** 19.00–24.00 Mon–Fri mid-June–mid-Sept; only weekends & bank holidays in winter

The Governor's Palace at the summit holds a small archaeological museum with Roman coins, artefacts and pottery fragments bearing Arabic motifs. Nearby is a refreshment stand for drinks and ice cream.
Palace and museum 🕿 96 642 0656 🕑 10.00–13.30 & 17.00–20.30 summer; 10.00–13.30 & 15.00–18.00 winter ❶ Admission charge includes entry to the archaeological museum and the ethnological museum in town

Museu Etnològic (Ethnological Museum)
Denia's past prosperity from the raisin industry is chronicled in this museum, with photographs and displays portraying the work and lifestyle of that era.
🄰 Calle Cavallers 1 🕑 10.30–13.00 Tues–Sat, closed Sun evening and Mon ❶ Admission charge (combined ticket including entry to the castle)

Safari Park Vergel
Lions, tigers, jaguars, wolves and many other animals roam this small safari park. You can also see huge reptiles, parrots, exotic birds and dolphin-and-seal shows. Horse and camel rides and other attractions.
🄰 On the Vergel–Pego road 🕿 96 643 9808 🕑 10.00–19.00 summer; 10.00–17.00 winter ❶ Admission charge

Walking
Rising behind Denia is Mount Montgó (762 m/2,500 ft). You can explore it via two hiking routes (guides available from the tourist office 🄰 Plaza Oculista Buigues 9 🕿 96 642 2367 🌐 www.denia.net 🄴 denia@touristinfo.net). The Ruta Ermitas de Conquista takes you to three hermitages on the lower slopes on an easy two- to three-hour walk. The more difficult climb through El Montgó Natural Park to the top can take all day.

A third hiking route follows the coastline to the Torre del Gerro, an old watchtower above Les Rotes, a fairly easy, one- to two-hour walk. Les Rotes is noted for its excellent fish restaurants. There is also an old English cemetery there.

TAKING A BREAK

Drassanes £–££ ❶   Hailed as one of the best seafood restaurants in town, this is a busy place and popular with a local crowd – always a good sign. ⓐ Calle del Puerto 15 ❶ 96 578 1118 ❷ 12.00–16.00 & 19.30–24.00

Betibo (Betty Boop) ££ ❷   Lovely open-air bar with easy-on-the-ear music. ⓐ 3 km (1¾ miles) out of town at the bottom of the Denia–Jávea road ❶ 96 642 1261 ❷ 18.00–late; July and Aug only

Bona Plaja ££ ❸   This fish restaurant is right on the beach, good for a cool beer or lunch. In the evening there is flamenco or other entertainment. *Arroz negro* (black rice with calamares) is a speciality, or you can have a steak. ⓐ 3 km (1¾ miles) out of Denia (look for the signs) on Carretera Las Marinas, Playa las Marinas ❶ 96 578 2777 ❷ 12.00–15.30 & 19.00–24.00

El Poblet £££ ❹   Dine outside on the cool terrace at one of the Costa Blanca's best restaurants. Denia is famous for its prawns, and here they are expertly prepared with other fresh seafood and creative variations on traditional rice dishes. ⓐ Carratera Las Marinas km 2.5 ❶ 96 578 4179 ❷ 12.30–15.30 & 20.00–late Tues–Sun

Restaurante Tasca Eulalia £££ ❺   This is what Spanish food is all about. A *tasca* is an eating house that serves the traditional Spanish tapas, small servings of fish, meat or vegetables, as a gourmet delight to accompany a glass of wine or beer, or a larger portion (*ración*) to add to your table. Full of atmosphere and very popular with the locals. ⓐ Marques de Campo 39 ❶ 96 578 6479

Jalón Valley Vineyards

The Jalón Valley is the vineyard of the Costa Blanca. Each year growers produce 2.5 million litres (550,000 gallons) of wine. A local cooperative can be found in the village centre of Jalón, where you can sample the wines – a red wine similar to claret and the sweet, potent muscatel for which the region is famed – and purchase some at low prices. You can also stop by for tastings at individual *bodegas* (wine cellars) – and fill up your bottle for a song or try some at any bar.

The gentle scenery of the Jalón Valley makes for a pleasant drive. Lush grapevines cover the fields, and you may spot some *riu-raus*, the traditional arched porches used for drying grapes to make raisins. The valley also has a wealth of almond trees, and the many varieties of almond cakes and biscuits are another temptation to indulge.

THINGS TO SEE & DO

Almonds, grapes & raisins

Jalón (Xaló in Catalan) lies at the centre of the valley, a quiet town surrounding a huge church with a shiny silver dome. As far back as 1472, its residents sent their wines to the court of Valencia and began selling a new product that became an economic staple of the Marina Alta: raisins. Look out for the bakery called **La Vicentica**, which turns out tasty fresh bread and cakes – a good place to try the *cocas* (pizzas) and pastries typical of the area. Nearby are the pleasant agricultural villages of Llíber and Alcalalí, with main crops of grapes, oranges and almonds. Parcent was home to Spanish writer Gabriel Miró, who called his town 'a paradise between mountains'.

Fabulous views

From Parcent, follow the road into the mountains towards Tárbena and Callosa to reach the Coll de Rates (Rat's Tail Pass). This is one of the finest viewpoints on the Costa Blanca, with a panorama that sweeps across the Jalón Valley to Denia, Jávea and the sea.

⬤ *Harvesting in the Jalón Valley*

For more heady views, carry on towards Tárbena through spectacular mountain scenery. The town is surrounded by fruit trees, full of blossoms in the spring, and has a pretty parish church. Beyond the village at the top of the pass is another fantastic viewpoint looking across the peaks and valleys to the coastal high-rises of Benidorm.

You may want to try some of the area's famous *sobrasadas* (red) or *butifarres* (black) sausages, made to an ancient recipe.

Gata de Gorgos

Near the Jalón Valley, about 9 km (5½ miles) from Jávea, Gata de Gorgos is known for its wickerwork industry and you will find shops selling baskets, hats, cane furniture and other crafts. Near the train station is a guitar factory where you can see how guitars are made, and buy one at factory prices.

ⓐ Guitarras de CashiMira, Calle Estación 25 ⓣ 96 575 6320
ⓦ www.joancashirmira.es ⓛ 09.00–13.00 & 15.00–18.30 Mon–Fri

TAKING A BREAK

El Corral del Pato ££–£££ Meat *a la brasa* (grilled) is the speciality of this family-run restaurant in the countryside. Enjoy dishes such as duck with fruit or oven-braised lamb (best to order this in advance), accompanied by side dishes typical of the Marina Alta. ⓐ Just on the outskirts of Gata, on the road to Jalón ⓣ 96 575 6834 ⓛ 12.30–16.00 & 19.00–late Tues–Sun

Casa Parra £££ Friendly restaurant that offers excellent Valencian cuisine served in the small dining room or out on the terrace. Special dishes such as *cordero al horno* (baked lamb) can be ordered in advance and are well worth it. ⓐ Avenida Marina Alta 86, Gata de Gorgos ⓣ 96 575 6121 ⓛ 13.00–15.30 & 20.00–23.00

▲ Baladrar beach on Benissa's coastline

Benissa

Benissa, a traditional inland town, is easily reached from Calpe or Moraira. Its quaint Old Town centre has retained its medieval and Moorish architecture and is a lovely place to wander.

Tourist Information Office ⓐ Avenida País Valencia 1, at the lower end of town on the N332 towards Valencia. ☎ 96 573 2225 ⏱ 09.30–14.00 & 15.00–20.00 Mon–Sat (closes earlier in winter), 09.30–14.00 Sun. There is parking all around Plaza Jaume I, the central square in Benissa. Make sure you buy a ticket from the machines – the traffic wardens are vigilant.

BEACHES

Although Benissa is an inland town there are 4 km (2½ miles) of nearby coastline, stretching between Moraira and Calpe, that contains tranquil coves backed by high cliffs. The biggest and most popular is sandy La Fustera, which is a Blue Flag beach. The Platgeta de L'Advocat has a small marina, which is popular for fishing.

THINGS TO SEE & DO

WALKING TOUR

Start in Plaza del Portal by the Town Hall, where there is a map showing historic points of interest. The road alongside the Town Hall leads to Plaza Esglesia Vella, a beautiful tiled square with ceramic murals. Walk up the **Calle Puríssima**, where the medieval houses have Moorish-style tiled porches and *rejas* (iron grilles) over the windows, a protection against pirate attack. Do not miss the ceramic tiles that line the window sills and decorate the undersides of the balconies. You will soon pass the 15th-century Lonja, the old grain and silk exchange with its pretty arched façade. It is now a centre for changing exhibitions on history and culture.

A little further along is another stately building, the 18th-century Casa Torres-Orduña, now the municipal cultural centre and library.

Retracing your steps slightly, turn left up Calle Angel to the charming Calle Desamparados, a row of elegant medieval houses with family coats of arms, huge wooden doors and enough wrought iron to withstand the most determined pirates. Carry on up Calle Sant Tómas and Calle Santo Domingo to reach the **Convento de la Puríssima Concepción**, built in 1612 as a Franciscan monastery. In front is a pretty courtyard ringed with tiled Stations of the Cross. Ring the bell and the custodian will show you around the cloister, chapel and quirky little museum full of fossils, coins, stuffed birds, vestments and artefacts brought back by missionaries from around the world. 🕐 10.00–12.30 & 16.00–18.00. Walk back along Calle San José and Calle San Nicolas to Plaza Jaume 1, for a look at the huge white limestone **Cathedral of the Marina Alta**, which was built between 1902 and 1929. 🕐 Open for visits 11.00–12.00

Then take a well-earned rest and have a drink at one of the bars around the palm tree-shaded square – the friendly **L'Orxatería (£)** in Rei Jaume I Calle serves a tempting array of ice creams and deliciously refreshing *limón granizado*, lemon-flavoured crushed ice. ☎ 96 573 1947

TAKING A BREAK

Benissa is known for its rich handmade sausages. Look out for *morcilla*, a type of black pudding, *blancos*, white pork sausages, or *longaniza*, long pork sausages.

FIESTAS
Benissa fiestas start early on in the year, beginning with the three-week-long *Fira i Porrat de San Antoni*, a craft fair held in the streets of the Old Town in January. The fourth Sunday in April is dedicated to the town's patron saint, la Puríssima Xiqueta, with street parties and fireworks. The Moors and Christians take to the streets in the last week of June with mock battles, parades and bands.

Altea

The Tuesday morning market in Altea is the biggest on the Costa Blanca. It snakes along the waterfront under a canopy of stalls selling shoes, boots, leather goods, lace and embroidery, clothes, jewellery and assorted goods. Do not expect to find too many local handicrafts, though. You can get there by tour coach, under your own steam or by public transport.

Altea's Old Town is a steep upwards climb of over 200 steps from the waterfront, and you would be hard-pressed to combine it with an excursion to the market unless you are extremely fit and adventurous. However, this picturesque village is a delightful place for strolling, and merits a separate visit. At the summit is **Plaza de la Iglesia**. The parish church is crowned by one of the finest blue domes in the region. The sloping streets of immaculate whitewashed houses fan out like bicycle spokes, opening up sparkling views out across the tiled roofs to the sea. There are many restaurants, several *café terrazas* around the large church square and numerous small art galleries in the side streets.

◆ *Old Town square, Altea*

THINGS TO SEE & DO

Palau Altea Centre d'Arts

Altea's exciting new cultural venue linked to the University of Miguel
Hernandez. Ongoing exhibitions of the loaned works of famous artists,
international theatre groups and nightly music concerts by Europe's
finest soloists. Programme information Casco Antiguo s/n
🛈 96 688 1924 🅦 www.palaualtea.com 🕒 According to performances
and exhibitions

TAKING A BREAK

La Capella Bar-Restaurant £–££ A passageway beside the church leads
under a vine-covered arched trellis to a garden patio with a beautiful
mountain view. Dishes served up by this traditional kitchen include
sausages, paella, seafood, chicken and veal. ⓐ Calle San Pablo 1
🛈 96 688 0484

La Claudia ££–£££ A very trendy eatery just below Church Square where
you can enjoy an evening meal of light, superbly presented international
dishes while seated in the cool whitewashed interior dining space or,
preferably, out on the terrace which, from its hilltop vantage point,
boasts some of the most idyllic sea views on the Costa Blanca.
ⓐ Calle Santa Barbara 4 🛈 96 584 0816 🕒 19.00–24.00

Guadalest

Guadalest, perched on a rocky outcrop over 610 m (2,000 ft) high, is the most visited village on the Costa Blanca. Its white bell tower at the top of a slender granite mass is one of the region's most striking images. Crowned by the ruins of an old Arab fortress, Guadalest was built as a Moorish stronghold during the 8th century. The only access is through a tunnel in the rock, which is why the village remained unconquered.

The town lies both inside and outside the natural fortress. To reach the castle, its highest point, you must go through the Casa de Orduña.

Guadalest bell tower

The path winds up to the Castle Square and village cemetery. Parts of the castle were destroyed in the earthquake of 1644. On the streets below, the village square, with its statue of St Gregory (the town's patron) overlooks the aquamarine waters of the reservoir.

Although the crowds of visitors can make Guadalest seem like a theme park, nearly 200 people actually live in this picturesque village. During the day the cobbled streets become a sort of Arab bazaar selling souvenirs and local crafts. The women of the village make elegant shawls, ponchos, lace and embroidered goods. There are several curio museums for amusement, and a number of restaurants.

Bring your camera and make sure you have plenty of space left on your memory card, or bring a spare film. The drive through the Guadalest Valley is splendid, with terraced slopes of almond, olive and citrus groves giving way to pine forests. Guadalest is featured on many organised tours and excursions – ask your resort representative for details.

SHOPPING

Calle la Virgen, the road where the Museo Belén is situated, is lined with souvenir shops.

Casa Artesana Sells a wide range of craft gifts from expensive cotton tablecloths and tea sets to tiny eggcups, ceramic bowls and onion jars for a few hundred pesetas. 🅐 Calle la Virgen 4 🛈 96 588 5239

Casa de la Miel Offers a huge selection of locally produced honey, as well as brandies, nuts, honey soap and cosmetics. 🅐 At the far end of Calle la Virgen 🛈 96 588 5258

Regalos Levante This unusual, if pricey, gift shop sells everything from ET tables and models of Captain Hook to more easily transported ceramics, candlesticks, jewellery and oil lamps. 🅐 Plaza San Gregorio, at the exit to the castle 🛈 96 588 5327

THINGS TO SEE & DO

El Arca de Noe

Do not be put off by the rough road: this animal park, set on a ridge over-looking the Guadalest Valley, carries an overwhelming 'wow' factor for children and adults alike. Its purpose is to rescue wild animals from poor conditions such as circuses and ill-equipped zoos. There is an enormous variety, including a cross-eyed jaguar, pythons with bronchitis, albino deer, anteaters confiscated at customs at Alicante Airport, as well as Phillip the Lion, who now roams the mountainside (behind a fence!) after years of living in a 3 by 3 m (10 by 10 ft) cage in a travelling circus.
ⓐ Near the main Guadalest car park towards Benimantell ⓣ 96 597 2359
ⓛ 10.00–18.00 ⓘ Relies on visitors' donations.

Casa de Orduňa and castle

This grand mansion was built after the 1644 earthquake by the Orduňa family, state governors and guardians of the fortress. Its fine furnishings and artworks reflect the lifestyle of wealthy Spanish aristocrats of the 18th and 19th centuries.
ⓐ Calle Iglesia 2 ⓣ 96 588 5393 ⓛ 10.15–20.00 summer; 10.15–13.45 & 15.15–20.00 winter ⓘ Admission charge

Casa Típica and Ethnological Museum

Traditional village life is portrayed in this house museum with antique household implements and tools for producing flour, wine and olive oil.
ⓐ Calle Iglesia 1 ⓣ 96 588 5238 ⓛ 10.00–21.00 Sun–Fri summer; 10.00–18.00 winter ⓘ Admission charge

Fonts de l'Algar

The sparkling rockpools and waterfalls of the Fonts de l'Algar are a refreshing natural oasis formed by a tributary of the Río Guadalest (Guadalest River). In a lush valley filled with lemon trees and orange groves outside Callosa d'En Sarrià, the river alternates between cascades and clear pools, its banks lined with fragrant summer flowers. You can

walk around the trail, pausing for a dip in the icy waters beneath the falls, before popping into the little environmental museum, which shows how essential oils are obtained from plants for use in aromatherapy.
ⓐ 3 km (2 miles) from Callosa ❶ Admission charge

In need of refreshment? The **Restaurante El Algar de Don Joan (££)** specialises in paella and meat dishes, and you can hang out at the lovely big pool for free. ❶ 96 588 0491. A little further down, the same applies at Casa Marcos (pool open from 11.00 to 20.00 hours).

Young children will enjoy the **Museo del Tren**, a small museum containing a large model landscape punctuated by miniature trains roaring past the tiny houses, windmills and stations. ⓐ Next to Restaurante El Algar de Don Joan ❶ 96 588 0491 ❶ 10.30–13.00 & 17.00–21.00 May–Sept ❶ Admission charge

Historical Medieval Museum

A gruesome display of instruments of torture and capital punishment.
ⓐ Calle Honda 2 ❶ 96 588 5348 ❶ 10.00–21.00 summer; 10.00–18.00 winter ❶ Admission charge

Museo Belén/Museo de Antonio Marco (Town of Bethlehem Museum)

Exhibits scale models of Spanish architecture and miniature dolls' houses, constructed over 15 years using authentic materials.
ⓐ Calle la Virgen 2 ❶ 96 588 5323 ❶ 10.00–21.00 summer; 10.00–18.00 winter ❶ Admission charge

Museo de Microminiaturas/Museo Microgigante

Two museums, one in Old Town, one near the car park, reveal incredible creations such as an ant playing a violin and famous artworks painted on a grain of rice.
Museo de Microminiaturas ⓐ Calle Iglesia 5 ❶ 96 588 5062.
Museo Microgigante ⓐ Calle del Sol 2 ❶ 96 588 5062 ❶ Both open 10.00–21.00 summer; 10.00–18.00 winter ❶ Admission charge

⬥ *The fortress ruins of Guadalest*

Museo Moros y Cristianos (Moors and Christians Museum)

The best of the brightly coloured silks, elaborate headgear and sequinned costumes of the annual Moors and Christians festivals are displayed here, along with a history and photographs of these important fiestas.
ⓐ 1.5 km (1 mile) before Guadalest on the Callosa d'En Sarrià road
ⓘ 96 588 5322 ⏱ 10.00–19.00 ❶ Admission charge

TAKING A BREAK

Cafetería Levante £–££ Pop in here for a sandwich, coffee and cake, or a light lunch of the omelette, salad and chips variety. ⓐ Plaza San Gregorio 7 ⓘ 96 588 5014

L'Hort ££–£££ This friendly, efficient restaurant serves high-quality, appetising food on a pretty terrace with a wonderful view.
ⓐ Calle la Virgen 1 ⓘ 96 588 5269 ⏱ 12.30–16.30

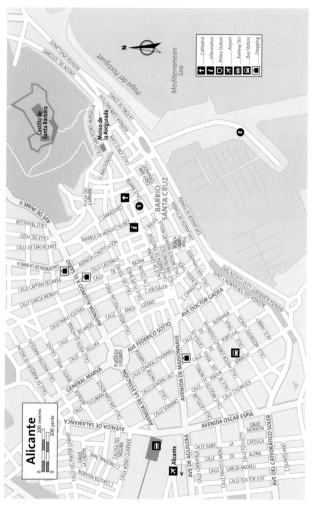

Alicante

Alicante, the provincial capital and gateway to the Costa Blanca, deserves more than a visit to the airport. Try to find some time during your holiday to take a tour of this dynamic and historic city.

Iberians, Greeks and Romans had settlements at Alicante. The present city was built by the Moors in the 8th century. It flourished during medieval times, becoming the third-largest seaport in Spain. Alicante has other beaches, museums and monasteries beyond those listed here.

Tourist office: Avda Rambla de Méndez Núñez 23 ☎ 96 520 0000; Alicante Airport ☎ 96 691 9100; Portugal 17, Bajo ☎ 96 592 9802

THINGS TO SEE & DO

Barrio Santa Cruz

The narrow streets of Alicante's old Moorish *barrio* (quarter) provide a glimpse of Spanish life away from the beach bars. Santa Cruz is a crumbling maze of roof terraces and flower-filled balconies with washing flapping in the breeze while women natter on doorsteps. Everywhere you turn you catch glimpses of glittering fountains tucked away in pretty squares.

Castillo de Santa Bárbara (Castle of Santa Bárbara)

This 16th-century military fort, built by King Philip II, is perched like a giant eagle's nest 180 m (590 ft) above the city. There are magnificent views of the town, beach and bay from several levels – don't forget your camera. There is also a small museum of ancient artefacts and pottery and a new exhibition of paintings, sculpture and photography from the collection of the Institut Valencia d'Art Modern. It is a long, hot walk up to the castle – to save your legs, you can take a lift up (and down) from the end of Avenida J.B. Lafora (look for a tunnel entrance cut into the wall).

🕐 10.00–19.30 summer; 09.00–18.30 winter ❶ Entrance to the castle is free, but there is a moderate charge for the lift

⏶ *Explanada de España*

Explanada de España

Alicante's waterfront promenade is one of the most beautiful in Spain. The broad path of wavy, marble tiles runs between towering palms, making for a shady place from which to observe Spanish city life over a coffee or an ice cream.

Museo de la Asegurada (Museum of 20th-century Art)

This spacious museum is a pleasure to visit, with enough works by famous artists such as Joan Miró, Max Ernst, Pablo Picasso, Salvador Dalí and Marc Chagall to make it a worthwhile trip for anyone with even a passing interest in modern art.

ⓐ Plaza de Santa María 3 ① 96 514 0959 ① 10.00–14.00 & 17.00–21.00 Tues–Sat summer; 16.00–20.00 winter; 10.30–14.30 Sun all year ① Admission free

Playa del Postiguet
If you are in need of a cool down, the sandy Playa del Postiguet beach is within easy reach of the town.

TAKING A BREAK

Santa Faz £ ❶ Just a few steps off the Rambla you'll find this authentically Spanish bar-cum-café, which does great pastries and *churros* for breakfast, and cheap and cheerful tapas for lunch, washed down with a glass of local wine. A firm favourite with the residents of central Alicante and almost always packed out. ⓐ Calle Mayor 4 ❶ 96 520 5302

SHOPPING
Artesania Reasonably priced ceramics in modern and traditional designs – pick up a pot for *ajos* (garlic) or *arroz* (rice) or beautiful bowls and cruet sets. ⓐ Avenida Alfonso X El Sabio 15 ❶ 96 514 0139 ⏱ 10.00–14.00 & 18.00–21.00, closed Sat afternoon & Sun

El Corte Inglés Open continuously from 10.00 to 21.30, this spacious department store is a joy to shop in, with everything from quality fashions to homewares and great air-con. Restaurant and toilets are on the top floor. ⓐ Calle Maisonnave 53

Markets:
- Alicante's local market. ⓐ Plaza Campoamor (near the bullring) ⏱ Thur & Sat mornings
- Central Market's mosaic-fronted food market is great to wander through, just to see all the shiny, sun-ripened produce on offer. ⓐ Avenida de Alfonso X El Sabio ❶ 96 514 0763 ⏱ Mon–Sat mornings only

The most secure parking in Alicante is in the attended parking enclosure on Explanada de España opposite the Marina. Shoppers can also use the underground car park of El Corte Inglés.

La Dársena ££–£££ ❷ Set alongside the marina and shaped like a ship, this smart restaurant specialises in over 200 kinds of rice dishes. Fresh seafood here is also superb. ⓐ Marina Deportiva 6, Puerto Muelle de Levante ❶ 96 520 7589 Ⓦ www.darsena.com ❶ 12.30–15.30 & 20.00–24.00

Alicante's **Hogueras de San Juan**, in the last week of June, is one of the region's most famous fiestas; a week-long celebration of summer, with fireworks, parades, all-night parties, live music and bullfights, culminating in the Nit del Foc (Night of Fire), when bonfires burn throughout the city.

AFTER DARK

The Paseo Marítimo, Alicante's portside promenade, is great for summer-time entertainment. From mid-July to the end of August, there is an international festival of music, dance and theatre including jazz, ballet, symphony orchestras and opera, all in the open air. As well as the shows, the port is a focal point for lively restaurants, bars and discos, such as the Irish pub **O'Hara's** and **Feelings Nightclub**. The bars in the Barrio Santa Cruz, east of the cathedral, also come alive at night.

Elche

A former Roman colony, Elche boasts the largest palm grove in Europe, with over 300,000 palm trees in and around the city, which are protected by law. Situated on the banks of the Vinalopó River, it is home to over 200,000 inhabitants, although holidaymakers will want to concentrate their attentions on the Old Town, which has plenty of interesting museums and historical buildings to dip in and out of and a myriad of palm tree-shaded squares.

Elche is the centre of Spain's shoemaking industry. Ask at the tourist office on the edge of the Parque Municipal (❶ 96 545 2747 ⓦ www.turismedelx.com) about factories that offer guided tours and the chance to buy shoes at factory prices. ❶ 10.00–19.00 Mon–Fri, 10.00–14.30 Sat, 10.00–14.00 Sun

THINGS TO SEE & DO

Baños Arabes
The remains of the Arab baths underneath the convent date back to the 12th century, when they were used by the Muslims to purify their bodies before prayer. The baths were closed in 1270, when a convent was established here after the arrival of Christian conquerors, and were later used for storage. A short soundtrack in English explaining the history is available on request.
ⓐ Convento de la Mercé, Plaça de la Mercé ❶ 96 545 2887 ❶ 10.00–13.30 & 16.30–20.00 Tues–Sat, 10.30–13.30 Sun ❶ Admission free

Basilica de Santa María
The 17th-century basilica with its blue-tiled dome is the focal point of Elche's Old Town. The inside is very elaborate – take a look at the ornate ceiling where a hatch allows participants in the mystery play (see Fiestas, page 80) to appear from the sky.
ⓐ Plaça Santa María ❶ 96 545 1540 ❶ 07.00–13.30 & 17.30–21.00; Tower 11.00–18.00 ❶ Admission charge (Tower)

Huerto del Cura

This glorious garden is filled with the palm trees that made Elche famous. There are cacti, terrapin and goldfish ponds and beautiful flowers. Look out for the unusual imperial palm with eight palm trees growing from a single stem. There is also a copy of the *Dama de Elche*, which is the symbol of Elche, the bust of a woman that was discovered at La Alcudía, 2 km (1¼ miles) south of Elche, in 1897.

ⓐ Porta de la Morera 49 ❶ 96 545 1936 🕒 09.00–20.30 summer; 09.00–18.30 winter ❗ Admission charge

Museo Arqueológico

Situated in a former military fortress, this museum holds a collection of local pottery, statuary and ceramics – lookout for the 2nd-century *Sleeping Eros* and the headless *Venus de Ilice* from Roman times.

ⓐ Palacio de Altamira ❶ 96 665 8203 🕒 10.00–13.30 & 16.30–20.00 Tues–Sat, 10.00–13.30 Sun ❗ Admission charge; free on Sun

FIESTAS

The most important festival in Elche is the **Misteri d'Elx**, a medieval religious play portraying the death of the Virgin and her assumption into heaven. It is staged annually in the basilica on 14 and 15 August. The performance is very professional, a colourful drama of singing, music and angels descending from the basilica's ceiling. There is also a special performance of the mystery play during the Festival of Medieval and Renaissance Theatre and Music, which takes place at the end of October/beginning of November in every even-numbered year.

The **Diumenge de Rams** (Palm Sunday) procession is also a spectacular sight, when the town's inhabitants parade through the streets carrying white palm branches.

Museo Municipal de la Festa

This museum is dedicated to Elche's famous mystery play portraying
the death and assumption of the Virgin Mary (see Fiestas, opposite).

The focal point of the museum is the audiovisual display about the
history and legends surrounding the death of the Virgin and a chance to
see the technical tricks that allow the play to be performed in Elche's
basilica; an English soundtrack is available.

ⓐ Calle Mayor de la Vila 25 ❶ 96 545 3464 🕒 10.00–13.30 & 16.30–20.00
Tues–Sat (17.00–21.00 July–Aug), 10.00–13.00 Sun ❶ Admission charge

Río Safari Elche

Take a 20-minute boat ride around this safari park for close-up views of
tigers, giraffes, hippos, monkeys and other furry and feathered friends.
There are also seal shows, a reptile house, an aquarium and camel
rides, as well as a go-kart track, slides and swings, trampolines and a
swimming pool; all great for kids.

ⓐ On the Elche–Santa Pola road (C-3317) about 4 km (2½ miles) before
Santa Pola ❶ 96 663 8288 Ⓦ www.riosafari.com 🕒 10.30–20.00
summer; 10.30–18.00 winter ❶ Admission charge

While you are walking around Elche, look out for palm trees with
their branches tied together in order to bleach them (the restricted
flow of sap causes the branches to die and turn white) so that they
can be cut down and distributed throughout Europe to make crosses
for Palm Sunday.

TAKING A BREAK

Cafetería Africa £ Take a break from sightseeing in Elche at this
pleasant, down-to-earth café opposite the basilica. Despite the
pretty location, the fresh, tasty sandwiches and burgers remain
reasonably priced.

○ *Río Segura runs through Orihuela*

Orihuela

Capital of the Alicante province, Orihuela is the town tourism forgot. The town lies 22 km (14 miles) from Murcia, its quiet streets are lined with orange trees, and shady squares are fringed with ornate palacios and crumbling façades. The elegant churches and buildings bear witness to the town's rich heritage as an affluent university and cathedral city, before Alicante usurped Orihuela's position as regional capital in the 19th century, making it a pleasant place to soak up some Spanish culture.

THINGS TO SEE & DO

Aquopolis

If the children have seen one church too many, pep them up with a visit to the Aquopolis water park on the northwest outskirts of Torrevieja. It contains all the usual kamikaze slides, a wave pool, a slow river ride and water amusements for children (including big children) of all ages.

ⓐ Finca de la Hoya Grande s/n, Torrevieja ☏ 96 571 5890 ◷ 11.00–19.00 mid-June–Aug; 11.00–19.00 until late Sept

Cathedral

This magnificent Catalan Gothic cathedral was built on the site of an ancient mosque at the beginning of the 14th century. It contains attractive cloisters, unusual spiral rib vaulting and a museum. The highlight, however, is Velázquez's painting *The Temptation of Saint Thomas*; this place is well worth a visit.

ⓐ Calle Ramón y Cajal ◷ 10.00–13.00 & 17.00–19.00 Tues–Sat, 10.00–14.00 Sun

Pop into the tourist office for a map at Calle Francisco Diez 25 (☏ 96 530 2747) – it is worth going anyway just to admire the gorgeous tiled entrance hall and floor of the Palacio Rubalcava, where it is based. ◷ 09.00–14.30 Mon–Fri

EXCURSIONS

Colegio de Santo Domingo

This former Dominican monastery and university is now a private school, but you can ring the bell and wander through the two glorious cloisters – the outstanding Renaissance cloister around a palm-tree garden and the baroque university cloister built 1727–37. Visit the refectory for a look at the 18th-century ornamental frieze made from Manises tiles.

ⓐ Calle Adolfo Clavarana 1 ⓛ 10.00–13.30 & 16.00–19.00 Tues–Fri, 10.00–14.00 & 16.00–19.00 Sat, 10.00–14.00 Sun ❶ Admission free

Golf

The coastal area south of Torrevieja is well equipped with golf courses, with **Villamartín** (ⓣ 96 676 5170) inland from the Playa Zenia and **Las Ramblas** (ⓣ 96 532 2011) and **Campoamor** (ⓣ 96 532 0410) a little south.

Museo Semana Santa (Easter Week Museum)

This museum houses the religious processional effigies that are paraded through the streets as part of Easter celebrations. The most interesting one, the she-devil and skeleton ('La Diablesa'), by 17th-century sculptor Nicolás de Bussi, is kept in the Museo de San Juan de Dios.

ⓐ Calle del Hospital, just before the Centro de la Salud ⓛ 10.30–13.30 daily, then 17.00–20.00 Mon–Sat summer; 16.30–19.00 winter ❶ Admission free. The *Diablesa*, which is not allowed into churches, is paraded through the streets on Easter Sunday to scare wrong-doers into repenting. ⓐ Calle Ballesteros Villanueva 1 ⓛ 10.00–13.00 & 16.00–18.00 Mon–Fri, 10.00–13.00 Sat ❶ Admission free

TAKING A BREAK

Café Bar Casablanca £ This cheap, cheerful but basic joint next to the Church of St Justa may be the only place open in the old part of town in the heat of the afternoon. Reward it with your custom. Choose from a selection of inexpensive tapas at the zinc bar or order a full meal washed down with a glass or two of local wine. ⓐ Calle Meca 1 ⓣ 96 530 1029 ⓛ 07.00–17.00, closed weekends Aug

Murcia

Murcia is a large city at the heart of the Segura river valley. Surrounded by fertile agricultural land laden with orange orchards, lemon groves and vegetable fields, it was founded by the Moors in the 9th century and has prospered as an agricultural and commercial centre ever since. The city of Murcia itself is a delightful combination of flamboyant baroque architecture, picturesque squares and a medieval old quarter, yet it has enough modern shops to keep the most determined bargain hunter happy.

The town's friendly and efficient tourist office is situated opposite the cathedral. ⓐ Plaza de Belluga ☎ 96 835 8600 🕐 09.00–14.00 & 16.00–20.00

THINGS TO SEE & DO

Balneario de Fortuna

If it is too hot to be tramping around museums and monuments, then indulge in the little spa village of Balneario de Fortuna, 25 km (15½ miles) northwest of Murcia. At one of the three Balneario de Fortuna hotels, you can relax with a thermal massage or soak in a spa bubble bath at affordable prices. Treatments are available mornings only (08.00–13.00) and it is best to book (☎ 96 868 5011). There is also a wonderful outdoor swimming pool where you can spend the day. 🕐 10.00–21.00 summer; 10.00–17.00 winter ❶ Admission charge

Casino de Murcia

A stroll through the faded opulence of this casino, built between 1847 and 1901, is like stepping back in time. As you enter, you half expect gentlemen with waxed moustaches, fat cigars and smoking jackets to be brandishing cues in the darkly wooded billiard room, or taffeta-clad ladies to exit from the most ornate powder room you will ever see – huge gilt mirrors, a painted ceiling and magnificent upholstery. The elaborate ballroom, with chandeliers of French crystal, sumptuous

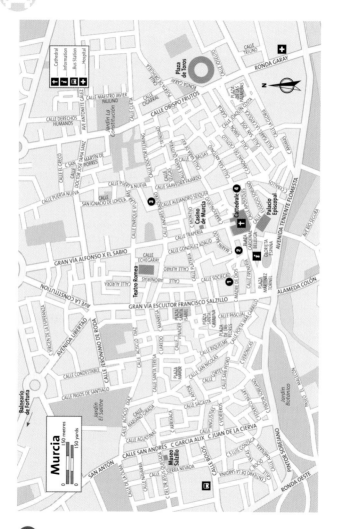

fabrics, gilt and carvings, is worth a look, too, as is the entrance hall, a masterpiece of intricate tile work and decoration.

ⓐ Calle Trapería 22 ☏ 96 821 5399 Ⓦ www.casinomurcia.com
🕒 09.30–21.00 ❶ Admission charge

If you are driving, it is a good idea to use the parking of the department store, El Corte Inglés, where the car park will keep your vehicle cool and it is only a ten-minute walk to the Old Town.

Cattedrale (Cathedral)

Murcia's grand cathedral, begun in 1394, encompasses a variety of styles, with a strong Gothic influence inside and baroque curves, carvings and pillars adorning the façade outside. The cathedral museum contains a wood-carving of San Jeronimo holding a cross and a skull by Murcia's most famous son, Francisco Salzillo.

ⓐ Plaza Hernández Amores 🕒 10.00–13.00 & 17.00–19.00
(20.00 in summer) ❶ Admission free, charge for the museum

Museo Salzillo (Salzillo Museum)

This museum houses the religious sculptures of Murcia-born Francisco Salzillo (1707–83), Spain's most famous 18th-century sculptor. Set out in a beautifully frescoed chapel, nine groups of huge, carved figures depict biblical scenes, which form an important part of the Easter Week celebrations.

Plaza San Agustín 3 96 829 1893 www.museosalzillo.es
09.30–14.00 & 17.00–20.00 Tues–Sat, 11.00–14.00 Sun Admission charge

The Museo Salzillo is a good 20-minute walk from the cathedral – on a hot day, it is worth flagging down a taxi.

TAKING A BREAK

La Abadía de San Antonio ££ ❶ Lovely traditional tapas bar in an attractive arched building. Calle Sociedad 1 96 821 1091 11.00–late

Café Roma ££ ❷ The best of a row of cafés on the main square, and a tourist refuge in the heat of the afternoon siesta. Munch on pastas, salads, tapas and sumptuous desserts in the cool interior or outside while admiring the intricate façade of the cathedral. Plaza Cardenal Belluga 6 96 822 2801 08.00–24.00

Mesón El Corral de José Luis ££ ❸ Indulge in a variety of tapas, from fresh anchovies and squid to stuffed peppers, artichokes and mushroom kebabs in this beautifully tiled authentic Spanish restaurant, or choose a Murcian speciality from their extensive à la carte menu. Plaza de Santo Domingo 96 821 4597 12.00–16.00 & 19.00–24.00

Rincón de Pepe ££–£££ ❹ Two excellent options in Murcia's smartest hotel: a superb selection of tapas is served in La Muralla tapas bar, built around a part of an ancient Arabic wall. The elegant formal restaurant serves superb grilled meats, fresh seafood and regional dishes.
NH Rincón de Pepe, Calle Apóstoles 34 96 821 2239 Restaurant 13.00–16.00 & 20.30–24.00; café 16.00–02.00

Cartagena

Cartagena was founded by the Carthaginians in 227 BC before spending several centuries under Roman domination. The city's location around a natural harbour, combined with the riches from the surrounding silver mines, made it a highly prized possession. Nowadays it is a mixture of modern industrial city, naval dockyards and a very attractive *casco antiguo* (old quarter), which is a blend of Roman ruins, elegant churches and some wonderful modernist buildings.

THINGS TO SEE & DO

Calle Mayor

If you are in Cartagena for the evening, join the throng of locals in the ritual pre-dinner stroll up and down this street, browse the shop windows, and stop off for an ice cream or aperitif at one of the many bars or cafés.

◐ *The world's oldest submarine in Cartagena*

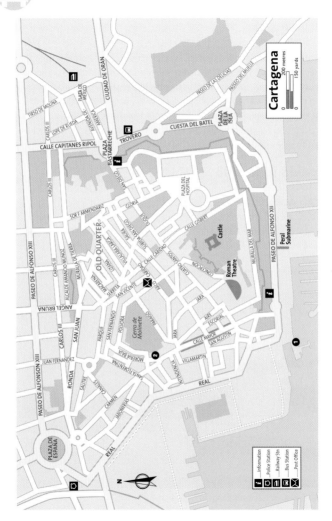

Cartagena

0 ___ 200 metres
0 ___ 150 yards

Information
Police Station
Railway Stn
Bus Station
Post Office

Old Quarter

Stroll through the Old Quarter to admire the marvellous façades of the modernist buildings. Look out for the **Palacio de Aguirre** on the corner of Plaza Merced with its shiny domed tower and rococo ceramic motifs – the bees on the tower signify diligence and industry. The Gaudí-inspired **Maestre House**, now a bank, in Plaza San Francisco has beautiful wrought-iron and stone balconies, and the richly decorated **Llagostera House** in Calle Mayor is also worth a look.

Peral Submarine

Down by the port is the original model of what Cartagena claims to be the first submarine, built by local inventor Isaac Peral in 1888.

Teatro Romea (Roman Theatre)

This crumbling theatre was built in 3 BC. Nearby is the ruined, 13th-century Cathedral of Santa María. Bombarded during the Spanish Civil War, there are now plans to restore it.

🅐 Calle Soledad

FIESTAS

Cartagena has a programme of festivals throughout the year. In February, there is a lively carnival. Easter Week sees sombre processions and marching bands. One of the most important festivals is the ten-day Carthaginian and Roman fiesta in the second half of September, with mock battles, legions of marching Roman and Carthaginian troops, and fireworks. Both sides set up historical camps, with food and drink to reflect the era, then party the night away to the anachronistic sounds of modern dance music.

From around 10 July to the end of the month, there is an ethnic music festival in Parque Torres and Parque Artillería from 23.00 (admission charge). In the same period, you can enjoy a great atmosphere and good music for free – live bands often play at around 20.00 in the Plaza del Ayuntamiento, in front of the Town Hall.

The tourist office at Plaza Almirante Bastarreche (**☎** 96 850 6483) can supply a map of all the modernist buildings in Cartagena.

TAKING A BREAK

La Patacha ££ **❶** This fascinating restaurant fills a whole ship and is bedecked in brass bells, ships' wheels, barrels, rope and other nautical knick-knackery. As you might expect, seafood dishes crowd the menu. English-speaking staff. **ⓐ** Muelle Alfonso XII (ship docked by the harbour) **☎** 96 808 1448 **ⓦ** www.lapatacha.com **🕓** 12.00–17.00 & 20.00–24.00

La Tartana ££ **❷** Housed in one of Cartagena's modernista structures in the heart of the city centre, this eatery serves up a hearty menu of meat dishes, including veal, lamb and ox sirloin as well as tapas and seafood. **ⓐ** Puerta de Murcia 14 **☎** 96 850 0011 **🕓** 12.00–16.00 & 20.00–24.00

�》 *The narrow streets of Altea*

Food & drink

There is fabulous food to try all over the Costa Blanca, and meals are generally good value. Paella is the regional speciality, made of saffron rice prepared with seafood, chicken or vegetables. With fine cava, Spanish champagne (sparkling white wine), so affordable, you will be celebrating every night. The Spanish eat quite late, but in tourist areas you will be able to find places that serve meals throughout the day. Generally, lunch is served from 13.00 to 15.00 or 16.00 and dinner from around 19.30 until 23.00 or 24.00.

LIGHT LUNCHES & SNACKS

If you just want a sandwich, ask for a *bocadillo*, which is usually a hearty baguette made with tasty *serrano* ham, cheese and other fillings. *Cocas* are pies or mini pizzas, popular all over this region. They consist of a shortcrust pastry with various ingredients. A favourite is made with tuna fish, tomatoes and onions and looks like a Cornish pasty. There are also plenty of Western-style fast-food outlets and cafés that serve sandwiches and snacks.

TAPAS

These snacks were traditionally served as 'a little something' to accompany wine or sherry. They can range from nuts or olives to tasty morsels of ham and cheese, croquettes, squid or sardines. A selection of tapas makes a lovely light lunch. You can also ask for larger portions, called *raciones*.

RICE

Rice is the regional dish of Valencia province, prepared in countless variations in every town on the Costa Blanca. The most famous is *paella valenciana*, saffron rice with chicken and vegetables. Paellas are also made with fish, seafood and rabbit. Try *arroz negro*, a paella made with *calamares* (squid) and rice turned black from the squid's ink. *Arroz a banda* and *caldero* are rice dishes made with fish stock.

MEATS

Look out for barbecue restaurants that do meat *a la brasa* – cooked on a brazier. Choose from savoury pork chops, steaks or lamb cutlets. Other meats are prepared with delicious flavourings. Try *conejo al ajillo* (rabbit simmered in oil and garlic).

Sausages are particularly excellent, and some Costa Blanca towns are famed for their secret recipes, some of them very old. *Butifarres* are white and black puddings made with either meat or onions. The red *sobrasadas* are seasoned with aromatic herbs from the mountains.

If you are renting an apartment or villa, look for takeaway paella. Served in the paella pan, as in a restaurant, you pay a deposit to ensure

◯ *Various meats for sale at Alicante market*

the pan's return the next day. Spaniards eat paella for the midday meal, although most restaurants serve it in the evening. It is made to order and takes at least 30 minutes to prepare. The price is per person (minimum two people).

SEAFOOD

Seafood abounds on the Costa Blanca, and much of it is quite reasonably priced. Many fish are caught locally – try grilled red mullet or sardines, sea bass cooked in sea salt or fried baby whiting. *Langostinos* (giant prawns) are especially popular. A regional speciality is *zarzuela*, a kind of seafood stew. *Calamares* (squid) can be cooked in a sauce or is often deep-fried. Squeeze some lemon juice over it.

Another Alicante delicacy is salted fish, such as sardines, tuna, cod and fish roe, accompanied by pickled onions, capers and olives – a substantial aperitif.

TYPICAL DISHES TO TRY

- **Albondigas** Meatballs, usually served as tapas.
- **Alioli** Spread this thick garlic mayonnaise on toasted bread.
- **Gazpacho** In effect, liquid salad. Chilled soup made of puréed tomato, onion, cucumber, green pepper and garlic. Refreshing in hot weather.
- **Tortilla Española** (*tortilla de patatas*). Thick Spanish omelette made with potatoes. Served as tapas or in a *bocadillo* (sandwich).

BRITISH

If you're looking for a taste of home, most resorts can offer fish and chips, steak-and-kidney pie, ploughman's lunches and full English breakfasts, all washed down with a cuppa or a British beer.

DESSERTS

Watermelons, figs, pears and strawberries are among summer's cornucopia of fruit. There are delicious pastries, often made with almonds or honey. *Flan* (crème caramel), *helado* (ice cream) and *tarta* (cake) with fruit are also popular.

COFFEE & TEA

Tea is not a Spanish forte, but coffee-lovers are in for a treat. *Café solo* is strong and black, served in a small glass. *Café cortado* is also strong and served with a splash of milk or cream. *Café con leche* comes in a larger cup and is half coffee, half milk. If you find the *café solo* too strong (and too small), ask for *un café americano* – which is a larger version of the *café solo* with extra water added.

WINES, BEERS & SPIRITS

Spain produces excellent wines, beers and spirits, *jerez* (sherries) and *cava* (champagne-style sparkling wine). A good cava is Codorníu, and you will also recognise Freixenet, sold at home at twice the price. Both have *brut* (dry) and semi-dry varieties.

The Jalón Valley is famous for its muscatel grape, which produces a sweet, strong dessert wine of the same name.

There are plenty of the popular Rioja wines around, but be sure to try some of Alicante's own excellent *vino tinto* (red). *Viña Vermeta* is nice, with a hint of vanilla. Or visit a *bodega* (wine cellar) in the Jalón Valley, where you can try before you buy. In restaurants you can often order a jug of the *vino de la casa* (house wine).

San Miguel is a good and inexpensive Spanish lager. Spanish brandies are also good value, although they can be a little rough at the lower end of the price scale.

Many restaurants offer a *menú del día* (menu of the day). These can be excellent value – the three-course meal will usually include dessert, wine and bread.

Menu decoder

Aceitunas aliñadas Marinated olives

Albóndigas de pescado Fish cakes

Albóndigas en salsa Meatballs in (usually tomato) sauce

Alioli Garlic-flavoured mayonnaise served as an accompaniment to just about anything – a rice dish, vegetables, shellfish – or as a dip for bread

Bistek or **biftek** Beef steak; **poco hecho** is rare, **regular** is medium and **bien hecho** is well done

Bocadillo The Spanish sandwich, usually made with French-style bread

Caldereta A stew based on fish or lamb

Caldo A soup or broth

Carne Meat; **de ternera** is beef, **picada** is minced meat, **de cerdo** is pork and **de cordero** is lamb

Chorizo A cured, dry, red-coloured sausage made from chopped pork, paprika, spices, herbs and garlic

Churros Flour fritters cooked in spiral shapes in very hot fat and cut into strips, best dunked into hot chocolate

Cordero asado Roast lamb flavoured with lemon and white wine

Embutidos charcutería Pork meat preparations including **jamón** (ham), **salchichones** (sausages) and **morcillas** (black pudding)

Ensalada salad; the normal restaurant salad comprises lettuce, onion, tomato and olives.

Ensalada mixta As above, but with extra ingredients, such as boiled egg, tuna fish or asparagus

Escabeche A sauce of fish, meat or vegetables cooked in wine and vinegar, and left to go cold

Estofado de buey Beef stew, made with carrots and turnips, or with potatoes

Fiambre Any type of cold meat such as ham, **chorizo**, etc.

Flan Caramel custard, the national dessert of Spain

Fritura A fry-up, as in **fritura de pescado** – different kinds of fried fish

Gambas Prawns; **a la plancha** is grilled prawns, **al ajillo** is prawns fried with garlic, **Gambas con gabardina** is prawns deep-fried in batter

Gazpacho andaluz Cold soup (originally from Andalucía) made from tomatoes, cucumbers, peppers, bread, garlic and olive oil

Gazpacho manchego A hot dish made with meat (chicken or rabbit) and unleavened bread (not to be confused with **gazpacho andaluz**)

Habas con jamón Broad beans fried with diced ham (sometimes with chopped hard-boiled egg and parsley)

Helado Ice cream

Jamón Ham; **serrano** is dry cured, **iberico** is dry cured but far more expensive, and **de york** is cooked ham

Langostinos a la plancha Large prawns grilled and served with vinaigrette or alioli; **langostinos a la marinera** are cooked in white wine

Lenguado Sole, often served cooked with wine and mushrooms

Mariscos Seafood, including shellfish

Menestra A dish of mixed vegetables cooked separately and combined before serving

Menú del día Set menu for the day at a fixed price; it may or may not include bread, wine and a dessert, but does not usually include coffee

Paella Famous rice dish originally from Valencia but now made all over Spain; **paella valenciana** has chicken and rabbit;

paella de mariscos is made with seafood; **paella mixta** combines meat and seafood

Pan Bread; **pan de molde** is sliced white bread; **pan integral** wholemeal

Pincho moruno Pork kebab: spicy chunks of pork on a skewer

Pisto The Spanish version of ratatouille, made with tomato, peppers, onions, garlic, courgette and aubergines

Pollo al ajillo Chicken fried with garlic; **pollo a la cerveza** is cooked in beer; **pollo al chilindrón** is cooked with peppers, tomatoes and onions

Salpicón de mariscos Seafood salad

Sopa de ajo Delicious, warming, winter garlic soup, thickened with bread, usually with a poached egg floating in it

Tarta helada A popular ice-cream cake served as dessert

Tortilla española The classic omelette, made with potatoes and eaten hot or cold; if you want a plain omelette ask for a **tortilla francesa**

Zarzuela de pescado y mariscos A stew made with white fish and shellfish in a tomato, wine and saffron stock

LIFESTYLE

Shopping

Spain is noted for its leather goods, and Benidorm and Denia have shops with fine selections of coats, jackets, handbags, wallets, belts, luggage and shoes.

HANDICRAFTS

Lladró handmade porcelain statues and figurines are famous worldwide and are made near the Costa Blanca, on the Costa Azahar. They are on sale throughout the resorts and at the factory outlet store in Valencia (see page 50). Look for lace tablecloths, shawls and crochet work in Guadalest, cane and basketwork in Gata de Gorgos, and pottery in Elche.

If you would like to try your hand at making paella when you get home, you can find a paella pan at *ferreterías* (hardware stores) and street markets.

🔺 *Try markets for souvenirs*

FOOD & DRINK

- **Almonds**, **honey** and **chocolate** are other regional food specialities that are nice to take home.
- **Muscatel** is a very sweet dessert wine made locally in the Costa Blanca region. Spanish *cavas* (sparkling wines) and table wines are bargains, both around the resorts and at the airport.
- **Turrón** is a sweet made of almonds and honey, produced in Jijona, a mountain village. There are many varieties. An inexpensive treat to pick up as a present.

The large supermarkets are a good place to find good wine at low prices. **Carrefour** hypermarket is located just off the Benidorm bypass.
🕐 10.00–22.00 Mon–Sat

MARKETS

Markets are generally held one day a week in towns throughout the Costa Blanca. They open at 08.30 and close at about 14.00. It is easy to find them as they form the focal point of the town on market days, particularly the fruit and vegetable sections. You can go to the markets at Altea and Calpe by tour coach; contact your tourist office for further details.

Markets around the Costa Blanca include:
- Monday   Denia, Callosa, La Nucia
- Tuesday   Altea
- Wednesday   Benidorm, Cartagena
- Thursday   Villajoyosa, Jávea, Alicante, Murcia
- Friday   L'Alfàs del Pi, Finestrat
- Saturday   Alicante, Calpe
- Sunday   Benidorm, La Nucia car boot sale

Children

Children are well catered for on the Costa Blanca. There are special excursions for children and families, such as the Castle Conde de Alfaz (see page 34) and there are plenty of playgrounds dotted about. Children are also welcomed in restaurants.

Those beaches that have clean, soft sand and shallow water are particularly good for children. They enjoy exploring the castles at Denia and Alicante and the boat trips from Benidorm to Calpe or Peacock Island (see page 30).

BENIDORM
Aqualandia

This thrilling water park is said to be the largest in Europe. Here you can ride the Rapids, take a Kamikaze Slide or venture into the Black Hole. The park is beautifully landscaped into the mountainside, with gardens, waterfalls, fountains, pools, sunbeds and picnic areas providing cool havens. Olympic divers dressed as comic clowns put on two or three shows a day. ⓐ Rincón de Loix, Benidorm ❶ 96 586 4006/7/8 Ⓦ www.aqualandia.net ⓔ aqualandia@aqualandia.net Ⓛ 10.00–17.30/18.00 May–Sept or Oct (depending on weather); until 19.00 or 19.30 July–Aug ❶ Admission charge

Funfairs and trains

The larger resorts have funfairs for younger children, with carousels, toy train rides and the like. Children (and their tired parents) will also appreciate the *trenes turísticos* (tourist trains) that tour around many resort areas (see Xàtiva, page 53).

Mundomar

Next door to Aqualandia (you can visit both on a combined ticket), the Costa Blanca's 'Seaworld' also has a colourful array of toucans, flamingos, bats and birds. Do not miss the beautiful Guacamayo, a huge blue parrot from Brazil. Dolphins perform twice a day in the dolphinarium, and the

parrots and sea lions also put on a show. ❷ Rincón de Loix, Benidorm
❶ 96 586 9101/2/3 Ⓦ www.mundomar.es ❸ mundomar@mundomar.es
🕔 10.00–18.00 Oct–Apr; until 18.30 May–mid-July; until 20.00 mid-
July–Aug; until 18.30 Aug–Sept ❶ Admission charge

For unique souvenirs, visit the gift shop at Mundomar. It has a great
selection of ecological T-shirts, stuffed toy turtles and walruses, beautiful
baskets, crystal dolphins and wind chimes made of wood and shells.

Terra Mítica
This giant theme park recreates the ancient civilizations of Rome, Greece,
Egypt, Iberia and the Barbary Coast (see page 28). The newest attraction
is a water-borne journey of the 'Rescue of Ulysses'. ❷ Access from the
A-7 (Exit 65-A) and the N-332 at Benidorm, plus regular bus and train
services ❶ 90 202 0220 Ⓦ www.terramiticapark.com

🔺 Dolphins perform at Mundomar

Sports & activities

BEACHES

The Costa Blanca is renowned for its crystal-blue water and fine, white sands. Beaches are clean and well maintained. Many have been given the Blue Flag mark of excellence, distinguishing them as environmentally sound, first-class tourist beaches. These include:

- **Alicante** San Juan, La Albufereta, Tabarca Island
- **Benidorm** Levante, Poniente and Mal Pas
- **Benissa** Cala Fustera
- **Calpe** La Fossa-Levante, El Arenal-Bol
- **Denia** Las Marinas, Las Rotas
- **Elche** Los Arenales, El Pinet
- **Finestrat** La Cala
- **Jávea** El Arenal, Las Aduanas del Mar (la Grava)
- **Moraira** El Portet, L'Ampolla
- **Santa Pola** Levante

In addition to the large public beaches, there are small beaches in hidden coves, beaches with dunes, and beaches with pine forests or palm trees; often found down tracks marked 'Playa' or 'Cala' off main roads.

There is little natural shade on most beaches, so be prepared to pay for rented sun parasols.

GO-KARTS

One of the best tracks lies between Benidorm and Villajoyosa at **Karting Finestrat**. ⓐ Partida la Folla s/n, Finestrat, Benidorm ⓣ 96 579 2227 ⓛ 09.00–02.00 summer; 09.00–dark winter. There is also a small track at **Karting Laguna** in Jávea. ⓐ Behind tennis courts on Cabo la Nao road ⓣ 96 579 5711.

GOLF

There are 14 courses on the Costa Blanca. They are open year-round and have club and golf-cart rental. Some of the best include: Club de Golf

Don Cayo, a 9-hole course in Altea (☎ 96 584 8046); Club de Golf Jávea, a 9-hole course on the main Jávea–Benitachell road (☎ 96 579 2584); Club de Golf Ifach, a 9-hole course on the San Jaime residential estate on the Moraira–Calpe road (☎ 96 649 7114/6) and Club de Golf La Sella, an 18-hole course near Denia on the La Jara–Jesús Pobre road (☎ 96 645 4252).

HIKING

Above Benidorm is the Sierra Helada, which is over 400 m (1,312 ft) high and has the highest coastal cliffs in the whole of the Mediterranean. There are easy to moderate walking routes from town into the hills and across the ridge – these have expansive sea views. Ask at the tourist office for details.

HORSE RIDING

There are stables just outside Benidorm. Guides are available.
ⓐ Camino Cantera de Orozco ☎ 67 898 3119

WATERSPORTS

Many different watersports are on offer all along the Costa Blanca. Two main centres are Denia and Calpe. Denia has sailing, windsurfing, diving, fishing and rowing. You will find information about watersports at Calpés Nautical Club. Jávea and Benidorm have scuba-diving centres and in Benidorm you can learn to water-ski using the Cable Ski system at the Rincón de Loix end of the Levante beach (☎ 96 585 1386).

LIFESTYLE

Festivals & events

You can see the bright, frilly skirts and castanets of flamenco performers all around the Costa Blanca. This passionate form of music and dance has Arabic origins and developed in southern Spain. There are two styles. Bars, clubs and restaurants often feature the animated light style, with much hand-clapping, heel-drumming and finger-snapping. True flamenco is the mournful music of hardship that sprang from the mining villages, with the sombre dances passed down from generation to generation. Another regional variation is the *sevillanas*, a happy style of folk music and dance associated with fiestas.

Check out the English newspaper *Costa Blanca News* for tips on local events, activities and restaurants. It comes out once a week on Fridays.

FIESTAS

Spanish culture is celebrated in fiestas throughout the year. Many are religious festivals dedicated to a particular saint and are marked by street processions and church services. Other fiestas involve colourful feasts, fireworks and bull-running, with the celebrations lasting a week or more.

The Costa Blanca's most famous fiesta is **Moros y Cristianos** (Moors and Christians). It is celebrated in different towns throughout the year, though the finest is said to be at Alcoy on St George's Day (23 April). Townsfolk re-enact the battles of their ancestors; whether you masquerade as a Moor or a Christian is a matter of tradition, which is handed down from generation to generation.

Jávea and Villajoyosa hold their Moors and Christians festival in July, Denia in August, Altea in September, Benidorm in September/October and Calpe in October.

Another spectacular event is the *Fallas* (pronounced fye-yas) fiesta, when, after a week of festivities, giant satirical figures are set alight in the town squares on St Joseph's Day (San José), 19 March. Valencia's *Fallas* (12–19 March) is one of the biggest fiestas in Spain. Around 370 giant papier-mâché floats, up to 18 m (60 ft) high, take to the streets on the night of 15 March. There is a topical twist to the *ninots* (effigies), which represent politicians, bullfighters, members of the jet set and a whole variety of public figures. The culmination of the celebrations, the Festival of San José, takes place on 19 March, when the *ninots* are set alight, a symbolic burning of the old in order to welcome the spring. Others are held in Calpe, Denia and Benidorm. A similar event is Hogueras de San Juan (Bonfires of St John), held in Alicante on 24 June; smaller *hogueras* take place in Jávea, Denia, Benidorm and Calpe at this time.

🔺 *Moors and Christians festival*

LIFESTYLE

Each town celebrates the feast day of its patron. Among the highlights are Denia's Santísima Sangre fiesta in July, with the exciting Bulls at the Sea event (see page 57) where bulls are enticed to chase locals into the water, Calpe's Virgin of the Snows, on 5–6 August, with floats, parades and a bull-run in the streets, and Benidorm's patron saint festivities in November.

When you see the streets decorated with coloured streamers (bunting), it may mean that they have just had – or will soon have – a fiesta, so look out for posters with details of events.

● *Boats entering Denia harbour*

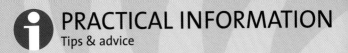

Accommodation

Hotel rates (double room rate in high season):
£ = below €50 ££ = €50–100 £££ = over €100

ALICANTE
Albir Playa £££
The strikingly modern white building of the 4-star Albir Playa contains contemporary interiors, some wonderful pools and a fine restaurant.
ⓐ Camino Viejo de Altea 51, Albir Playa ⓣ 96 686 4943
ⓦ www.albirplayahotel.com

BENIDORM
Gran Hotel Bali ££
At 186 m (610 ft) high, this is Europe's tallest hotel and Spain's highest building! There are sometimes great deals on its 776 modern rooms which, it goes without saying, enjoy some of the best views on the Costa Blanca. The building also houses a number of facilities that other hotels can only envy in silence. ⓐ Calle Luis Prendes, Benidorm ⓣ 96 681 5200
ⓦ www.granhotelbali.com

CALA DE FINESTRAT
Hotel La Cala £££
This sound option stands virtually on the beach. Some rooms have balconies where you can breakfast to the sound of the waves below.
ⓐ Avenida Marina Baixa 10, Cala de Finestrat ⓣ 96 585 4662
ⓦ www.hotel-lacala.com

CALPE
Hotel Solymar £££
Superbly situated right on the seafront, this smoked glass edifice contains 300 very well-appointed rooms. Those at the front have panoramic views of the beaches and the Penón de Ifach.
ⓐ Calle Benidorm 1, Calpe ⓣ 96 587 5055 ⓦ www.granhotelsolymar.com

DENIA

La Posada del Mar £££

Housed in a building that has stood on the seafront since the 13th century, this hotel offers extremely comfortable 4-star lodgings in a stylish Spanish environment of tiles, whitewashed plaster and beautifully carved wood. ⓐ Plaça de les Drassanes ⓣ 96 643 2966 ⓦ www.laposadadelmar.com

JÁVEA

Hotel Jávea ££

Situated just back from the Playa de la Grava at the far western end of the resort, this hotel has light and airy rooms, some with magnificent shoreline vistas. ⓐ Calle Pío X 5, Jávea ⓣ 96 779 5461 ⓦ www.hotel-javea.com

MORAIRA

Los Limoneros £££

A 3-star finca-style hotel centred around a great swimming pool illuminated at night. Five minutes' walk from the town centre and beaches. ⓐ Apartado de Correos 17, Moraira ⓣ 96 649 03 51 ⓦ www.loslimoneros.com

VALENCIA

Meliá Inglés £££

A beautifully appointed 3-star boutique hotel opposite the Ceramics Museum in a quiet part of the city centre. ⓐ Marqués de Dos Aguas 6 ⓣ 96 351 6426 ⓦ www.solmelia.com

VILLAJOUOSA

El Montiboli £££

Five-star opulence with stunning views from its cliff-top location. The outdoor pool is particularly impressive. ⓐ Ptda. El Montiboli ⓣ 96 589 02 50 ⓦ www.elmontiboli.com

Preparing to go

GETTING THERE

The least expensive way to get to the Costa Blanca is to book a package holiday with one of the leading tour operators specialising in Costa Blanca holidays. You should also check the travel supplements of the weekend newspapers such as the *Sunday Telegraph* and the *Sunday Times*. They often carry adverts for inexpensive flights, as well as classified adverts for privately owned villas and apartments to rent in the most popular holiday destinations. If your travelling times are flexible, you can also find some very cheap last-minute deals using the websites of the leading holiday companies. It always pays to shop around for the best prices.

By air

The Costa Blanca is served by Alicante's main international airport El Altet, 10 km (6 miles) southwest of the city. Some smaller carriers are making increasing use of San Javier Airport in Murcia with flights direct from Stansted. Scheduled flights to Alicante are operated by the Spanish national carrier Iberia Airlines, British Airways and easyJet.

These airlines offer online flight availability and bookings through their respective websites:

Ⓦ www.iberia.com, www.britishairways.com and www.easyjet.com

Many people are aware that air travel emits CO_2, which contributes to climate change. You may be interested in the possibility of lessening the environmental impact of your flight through the charity Climate Care, which offsets your CO_2 by funding environmental projects around the world. Visit Ⓦ www.climatecare.org

TOURISM AUTHORITY

Spanish National Tourist Offices around the world can send out detailed comprehensive information on all aspects of travel and tourism in the country.

London ⓐ PO Box 4009, London W1A 6NB ☎ 020 7486 8077
ⓦ www.tourspain.co.uk
New York ⓐ 666 Fifth Ave., 35th fl, New York, NY 10103 ☎ +1 212 265 8822
ⓦ www.spain.info
Toronto ⓐ 2 Bloor St West, Toronto M4W 3E2 ☎ +1 416 961 3131
ⓦ www.tourspain.toronto.on.ca

BEFORE YOU LEAVE

Make sure you and your family are up to date with the basics, such as
tetanus. It is a good idea to pack a small first-aid kit to carry with you.
Sun lotion can be expensive in the Costa Blanca so it is worth taking a
good selection of the higher factor lotions if you have children with you,
and do not forget after-sun cream as well. If you are taking prescription
medicines, ensure that you take enough for the duration of your visit –
you may find it impossible to obtain the same medicines in the Costa
Blanca. It is also worth having a dental check-up before you go if you
intend to stay some time.

Documents

The most important documents you will need are your tickets and your
passport. Check well in advance that your passport is up to date and has
at least three months left to run. All children, including newborn babies,
need their own passport, unless they are already included on the passport of the person they are travelling with. It generally takes at least
three weeks to process a passport renewal. This can be even longer in
the run-up to the summer months. For the latest information on how to
renew your passport, and the processing times, call the **Passport Agency**
on 0870 521 0410, or access their website ⓦ www.ukpa.gov.uk. All
Spanish nationals and foreign residents are issued with ID cards, which
must be produced on demand. You must carry your passport with you at
all times when in Spain.

If you are thinking of hiring a car while you are away, you will need to
have your UK driving licence with you. If you want more than one driver
for the car, the other drivers must have their licences too.

Insurance

Check that your policy covers you adequately for loss of possessions and valuables, for activities you might want to try – such as scuba-diving, horse-riding, or watersports – and for emergency medical and dental treatment, including flights home if required.

In January 2006, a new EHIC card replaced the E111 form to allow UK visitors access to reduced-cost, and sometimes free, state-provided medical treatment in the EU. For further information, ring EHIC enquiries line: ☎ 0845 605 0707 or visit the Department of Health website ⓦ www.dh.gov.uk

MONEY

You will need some currency before you go, especially if your flight gets you to your destination at the weekend or late in the day after the banks have closed. Traveller's cheques provide the safest way to carry money because the money will be refunded if the cheques are lost or stolen. To buy traveller's cheques or exchange money at a bank you may need to give up to a week's notice, depending on the quantity of foreign currency you require. You can exchange money at the airport before you depart. You should also make sure that your credit, charge and debit cards are up to date – you do not want them to expire in the middle of your holiday – and that your credit limit is sufficient to allow you to make those holiday purchases. Do not forget, too, to check your PIN numbers in case you have not used them for a while – you may want to draw money from cash dispensers while you are away. It is also wise to inform your bank that you will be using your card abroad.

Credit cards

Upmarket restaurants and department stores take credit cards, as do some of the petrol stations in main resort areas. Shops that accept credit cards will display the signs in their windows. Visa and MasterCard are most widely recognised. You will need cash in smaller restaurants, shops and towns.

Currency

Spain uses the euro, with €1 equalling 100 cents. Coins are €1, €2 and 1, 2, 5, 10, 20 and 50 cents. Notes are €5, €10, €20, €50, €100, €200 and €500. Use banks to exchange your pounds or traveller's cheques, rather than street kiosks where you may be charged a high commission fee. Before parting with your money, always ask how much you will receive in return less any commission or expenses.

Exchange bureaux

Opening hours of exchange bureaux are similar to those of shops. Rates of exchange can vary considerably. Note that some quoted rates may be based on the exchange of a minimum amount, and the service charge could be up to two per cent, or a set fee. You may also be able to exchange both cash and traveller's cheques at the reception desk at your hotel.

Tax

If you have bought a valuable item in Spain and you are flying out of the EU, you are eligible to a VAT refund of 13.8%. Visit the Global Refund website to learn about the various ways this can be done, and don't forget to keep all receipts etc. **Global Refund** Ⓦ www.globalrefund.com

CLIMATE

Take into account the time of year you are travelling when choosing clothes to take with you. Light casual wear is fine in summer, but you will need at least one warm item for the evenings, when temperatures can drop a few degrees. The Costa Blanca has little summer rainfall, but when it comes it can be heavy – a light plastic raincoat takes up very little room in your suitcase and you may be glad of it if caught in a summer storm. Avoid falling into the 'tourist trap' of taking clothes suitable only for the beach. Many nightclubs and restaurants will refuse bare chests, bikinis and shorts so make sure you pack some smart casual wear for the evenings.

BAGGAGE ALLOWANCE

Baggage allowances vary according to the airline, destination and class of travel, but 20 kg (44 lb) per person is the norm for luggage that is carried in the hold (it usually tells you what the weight limit is on your ticket). You are also permitted a single item of cabin baggage weighing no more than 5 kg (11 lb), and measuring 46 by 30 by 23 cm (18 by 12 by 9 in). You may only take one bag on board, but you can carry a coat too, if necessary. Large items – surfboards, golf-clubs, collapsible wheelchairs and pushchairs – are usually charged as extras and it is a good idea to let the airline know in advance if you want to bring these.

During your stay

AIRPORTS

The main gateway to the Costa Blanca is Alicante Airport, situated around 10 km (6 miles) to the southwest of the city, near El Altet. This relatively large terminal has the complete range of facilities you would expect to find, such as cafés, restaurants, a tourist information booth, car rental agencies and ATMs.

Airport Bus C-6, which runs every 40 minutes, shuttles passengers between the airport and the city centre (tickets: 1 euro, bought on board). Otherwise a taxi will cost around 20–25 euros. Buses run direct from the airport (some summer only) to other resorts and inland cities.
Ⓦ www.aena.es

COMMUNICATIONS
Post offices

These are called '*correos*' and exist in every town and village, but stamps can also be purchased in state tobacco shops, kiosks and shops that sell postcards. The usual services are available at post office counters, which are open from 10.00 to 14.00 Monday to Friday.

Telephones

There are numerous telephone booths dotted around where you can make calls with credit cards or using coins. Please be warned that if

> **TELEPHONES**
> To call the Costa Blanca from the UK, dial 00 34 then the nine-digit number – there's no need to wait for a dialling tone.
> To call the UK dial **00** and wait for the dialling tone to change. Then dial **44** (the country code) and the area code (minus the first 0) followed by the number. The country code for Ireland is **353**.

you are using coins, you will need lots of them. Calls can also be made from your hotel room, but this is an expensive option. Telefonica is the main telephone company and it generally has several kiosks in tourist areas where you can make metered calls and then pay an attendant afterwards. This is generally the most economical way of making telephone calls to the UK.

CUSTOMS

In Spain and all across the Costa Blanca, the siesta is common practice. It takes place from between 13.30 to about 17.00 and during this time all shops and museums close. Restaurants and cafés remain open, but will close between 17.00 and 21.00.

Spanish lunches are leisurely affairs – often lasting several hours. Consequently, Spaniards eat later in the evening. If you can't wait until after 21.00 to eat again, find some tapas to snack on before the restaurants close.

Spanish greetings involve an embrace and kisses on both cheeks.

DRESS CODES

The Spanish are pretty laid-back when it comes to how people choose to dress. You can wear shorts and T-shirts anywhere you like (museums, restaurants, etc.), though a bikini in a church may be slightly insensitive.

In July and August the Costa Blanca is incredibly hot with temperatures pushing 30°C (86°F) on a daily basis, and humidity high. On these days light cotton attire is advisable, preferably with long sleeves and trouser legs. A hat, sun block of at least protection factor 15 and sunglasses are a must.

ELECTRICITY

Spain operates under the 220 V (50 Hz) system so all appliances from the UK will work, but you will need a plug-adaptor kit, which you should be able to buy from your local high street. Less fiddly is a simple plug that adapts the standard UK 3-pin to the Spanish 2-pin earthed system. These are available in most Spanish hardware shops and from most UK airports.

If you are considering buying electrical appliances to take home, always check that they will work in the UK before you buy.

GETTING AROUND
Car hire & driving
Reasonably priced car hire is readily available and can often be booked through your tour operator before arrival. If you plan to drive it is worth taking out breakdown insurance with the AA or RAC. Since a disproportionately large number of private cars in Spain often have no insurance, consider fully comprehensive cover rather than plain third party risk. Remember that you will be driving on the right and the standard rule is to give way to traffic from the right, even on roundabouts. Drive carefully and observe all road signs. It is illegal to drive while using a handheld mobile phone, and drink driving penalties are severe. For lesser traffic offences, the Spanish Guardia Civil Traffic Police use an on-the-spot fine system and will impound your car if you are unable to pay up immediately.

Public transport
Public transport on the Costa Blanca is adequate and inexpensive in coastal areas but sparse inland. Buses and local train services (the *trenet*) link the coastal resorts. The Costa Blanca Tram runs between Alicante and Denia, roughly every hour from 06.00 to 21.00 or 22.00. It stops at many local stations along the way, including Benidorm, Altea, Calpe, Benissa, Gata and Denia with a change at Creueta. There is a price

---

EMERGENCIES
General EU emergency number ❶ 112
National police ❶ 091
Local police ❶ 092
Ambulance ❶ 061
Fire brigade ❶ 080

reduction for pensioners (you must show your passport). With the single track and the numerous stops, the 80-km (50-mile) journey takes 2 hours and 15 minutes and delays are common. See www.fgvalicante.com

Taxis

Taxis operate fixed tariffs only within town limits, so agree a price before you start a longer journey.

HEALTH, SAFETY & CRIME

Pharmacists in Spain are authorised to prescribe and supply many restricted drugs over the counter, so it is best to go there first before heading for the hospital or clinic. You will be expected to pay for non-emergency medical treatment even in a public hospital or clinic, although you might be able to reclaim the cost later on your travel insurance. Meanwhile, take obvious precautions to protect yourself from harm.

● Be safe on the beach and know the Blue Flag system

Health hazards Sunbathe sparingly and never between noon and 16.00, when the sun is at its hottest. Most upset stomachs are caused by a change to the rich Mediterranean diet, so do not overdo it until your body is accustomed to the food on offer.

Water Tap water is generally safe in Spain (most people blame the ice cubes instead of the alcohol), but bottled water (*agua mineral*) is inexpensive and plentiful.

Personal comfort & security

Every company, shop, restaurant and bar in Spain is required to hold a Complaints Register (*Libro de Reclamaciones*), which is regularly inspected by the local authorities. Complaints to the police are called '*denuncias*' and are accompanied by much form filling, especially in the case of theft. Be sensible and you will save yourself the trouble.

Your hotel will usually undertake your dry cleaning and laundry, although most holiday resorts have cleaners and laundrettes. Take enough clothes to save yourself the bother.

If you lose property in the street, try the local police station, although bar, restaurant and shop assistants will usually hold onto the item in case you return, so try to remember where you lost it. Do not 'lose' your bag or wallet accidentally by leaving it unattended.

In Spain, theft comes under two categories, '*robo*' and '*hurto*'. The former involves some form of bodily contact such as bag-snatching. The latter refers to stealing an unguarded item. Insurance companies

BEACH SAFETY

Take note of the flag system that advises you of swimming conditions.

- **Green** = safe bathing and swimming for all
- **Yellow** = caution – strong swimmers only
- **Red** = danger – no swimming

generally regard the latter as your own fault and refuse to pay compensation. Whatever the occurrence, always make a complaint (*denuncia*) to the police to support your claim.

Airports and resorts all over the world attract criminals, so be on your guard. If you are travelling with a tour group, take your luggage to the coach and stay with it until it is loaded. If you have chosen car hire, ask the desk representative to take you to your vehicle. They may refuse if they are busy, in which case decline all other offers of help from anyone loitering in the car park.

Leave all your valuables and spare cash in the hotel safe when leaving the hotel for the day. Your travel insurance may be void if you do not. The Costa Blanca crime rate is no worse and a lot better than many holiday destinations, but be alert and take sensible precautions as you would at home.

MEDIA

Many English-language programmes arrive via other channels, including the UK's Channel Five, CNN, Sky News and Eurosport. UK national newspapers are printed in Madrid and available on the Costa on the same day. The award-winning English language *Costa Blanca News* is published weekly and covers all local and national news, entertainment and notices of local fiestas and attractions. It is worth getting hold of a copy from a news-stand or hotel reception should you be spending more than a week or two on the Costa Blanca. Ⓦ www.costablanca-news.com Radio Onda Cero International (94.6 FM) and Spectrum Radio (88.2 FM) are English language radio stations with links to BBC World News throughout the day.

OPENING HOURS

Smaller shops and businesses in Spain follow the custom of the siesta, closing between around 13.30 and about 17.00 and then staying open until 19.30 or 20.00 Monday to Friday and closing Saturday afternoon and all day Sunday. Larger department stores and hypermarkets are usually open all day and some remain open on Sundays during the high

◐ *Eating alfresco is one of the pleasures of dining out*

season. Banks are open from 09.00 to 16.00 (except siesta time) Monday to Friday, with Saturday morning opening confined to the winter months, although most have 24-hour cashpoints (ATMs) that will accept UK cash cards. Pharmacies operate the siesta system, but will always display the address of an emergency 24-hour pharmacist in the area. Check out the opening times of places of interest with the local information office, especially for national and local public holidays, of which Spain has more than anywhere else in Europe. The Spanish eat late, with most restaurants opening at 21.00 and serving dinner until 24.00.

RELIGION

Spain is a Catholic country, although because of immigration and foreign residency, churches of most denominations abound. The British Anglican community is particularly strong on the Costa Blanca. The English-language newspaper *Costa Blanca News* carries a weekly list of church services for all denominations.

TIME DIFFERENCES

Mainland Spain is always an hour ahead of the UK and changes its clocks forwards and backwards according to GMT and BST with an hour added.

TIPPING

The Spanish service industry is reliant on tips, and it is customary to leave a few cents on the bar when you pay for a beer or coffee. In restaurants, the norm is around 15 per cent of the bill. Taxi drivers expect around 10 per cent.

TOILETS

Public toilets are virtually nonexistent throughout the Costa Blanca and you will usually have to rely on bars and cafés permitting you to use their facilities. Most rail and bus stations have toilets, and facilities everywhere are free to use and of a generally high standard.

TRAVELLERS WITH DISABILITIES

Many towns on the Costa Blanca have adopted excellent wheechair-friendly schemes by lowering pavements and removing barriers. Parking for visitors with disabilities is reserved in most areas and stringently enforced by the local police. Some resorts also provide special bathing facilities.

The following organisations can offer advice and assistance to travellers with disabilities:

Access Travel ⓐ 6 The Hillock, Astley, Lancs, M29 7GW, UK
ⓣ 01942 888 844 ⓐ www.access-travel.co.uk
Holiday Care Services ⓐ The Hawkins Suite, Enham Pl., Andover, SP11 6JS, UK ⓣ 0845 124 9971 ⓦ www.holidaycare.org.uk
SATH (Society for the Advancement of Travelers with Handicaps)
ⓐ 347 5th Avenue, New York, NY 10016, USA ⓣ 212 447 7284
ⓦ www.sath.org

ACKNOWLEDGEMENTS

We would like to thank all the photographers, picture libraries and organisations for the loan of the photographs reproduced in this book, to whom copyright in the photograph belongs:
Pablo Manzano Baena/Flickr.com page 44; Armando Suárez Cueto/Flickr.com page 120; Marc Di Duca pages 13, 14, 47, 89, 95; Echiner/Wikimedia Commons page 45; Age Fotostock/Superstock.com pages 18, 64; Kath Freer/ Spanish Tourist Office page 107; Paul Hampton/Dreamstime.com page 33; Hannu Liivaar/Dreamstime.com page 29; Pictures Colour Library pages 20, 37, 48, 67, 73, 76, 93, 100, 123; Rodriguillo/Wikimedia Commons page 10; Martin Röll/Wikimedia Commons page 82; Lesley Smith/vivathevalley.com page 62; Bernardo Valera/Dreamstime.com page 1; World Pictures/ Photoshot page 109; all the rest Thomas Cook Tour Operations.

Project editor: Alison Coupe
Layout: Donna Pedley
Proofreader: Jenni Rainford
Indexer: Marie Lorimer

Send your thoughts to
books@thomascook.com

- **Found a beach bar, peaceful stretch of sand or must-see sight that we don't feature?**
- **Like to tip us off about any information that needs a little updating?**
- **Want to tell us what you love about this handy, little guidebook and, more importantly, how we can make it even handier?**

Then here's your chance to tell all! Send us ideas, discoveries and recommendations today and then look out for your valuable input in the next edition of this title.

Email to the above address or write to:
HotSpots Series Editor, Thomas Cook Publishing, PO Box 227, Unit 9, Coningsby Road, Peterborough PE3 8SB, UK.